T0125315

THE LADY FROM AREZZO

ALFRED BRENDEL

The Lady from Arezzo

My Musical Life and
Other Matters

FABER & FABER

First published in 2019
by Faber & Faber Limited
Bloomsbury House
74–77 Great Russell Street
London wc1b 3da

Typeset by Faber & Faber Limited
Printed and bound by Livonia Print, Latvia

A CIP record for this book
is available from the British Library

isbn 978–0–571–35372–9

2 4 6 8 10 9 7 5 3 1

Contents

Introduction: A Mouth with Two Ears   1

Daniil Kharms *translated by Alfred Brendel*   4
   There was a Man
   Anecdotes from Pushkin's Life
   The Inventor Anton Pavlovič Šilov

Everything and Nothing: Dada 2016   7

Velimir Khlebnikov   39
   Incantation by Laughter
    translated by Paul Schmidt
   Incantation by Laughter
    translated by Vladimir Markov

The Lady from Arezzo   41

Charles Amberg   45
   Ich reiß mir eine Wimper aus
   Cabaret Song
    translated by Alfred Brendel

Joseph Haydn's *Seven Last Words*   47

Music: Light and Darkness   53

Schubert's *Winterreise*   61

Hans Arp   73
translated by Jeremy Adler
  From *Constellations*

Ernst Jandl   75
translated by Jeremy Adler
  Mountain Goat
  Sentence Mixture

Schumann's Piano Concerto: Some Notes on   79
  Performance

Christian Morgenstern   87
  The Knee
    translated by Alfred Brendel
  Das große Lalula
  The Does' Prayer
    translated by Max Knight

My Musical Life   91

Brief Nonsense Bibliography   119
The Authors of Nonsense Texts   121
Illustrations   123
Acknowledgements   125

Introduction: A Mouth with two Ears

'Utter nonsense!' is how some of us would react when the firm ground of common sense starts swaying under our feet. For many, nonsense is something plainly negative, bound to make us surrender even more willingly to the blessings of sense. I would like to proceed differently and propose that it is our habitual entanglement with sense, our dependence on sense, our enslavement by sense that makes the pleasures of nonsense truly evident.

Sense is restricted, tied to rules, and finite. Nonsense ignores such shackles. It tells us that sense, the normal, rational, real and 'natural', lives by its limitations. It is obligatory. Even when nonsense respects certain rules, it remains a game, opposed to conventions and the customary procedures of reason. We savour the temporary escape from the real and habitual. At the same time, our awareness of reality is sharpened.

The early German Romantics were fond of nonsense. Novalis dreamt of 'poems without any sense and coherence'. Similarly, Ludwig Tieck, the author of *Puss in Boots*, envisaged a 'book without coherence, full of contradictory nonsense'. (It was the Swabian writer Justinus Kerner who provided, with his *Reiseschatten*, one of the most enticing examples.) Later, Edward Lear and Lewis Carroll became the quintessential nonsense poets for many. But in fact, nonsense poetry had already been alive and well in the Middle Ages, if not in ancient Egypt. Around 1200, the German minstrel Reinmar the Old, besides being a *Minnesinger*, was paying tribute to a 'poetry of the impossible' ('mendacious poetry', *Lügendichtung*). In a text from the fourteenth century, a fierce battle between a hedgehog and a flying earthworm is arbitrated by a floating grindstone.

Being liberated from rational restrictions, nonsense leads into the infinite. One enters, if so inclined, a religious sphere.

In this volume, a few nonsense texts translated from the Russian and German are interspersed between my own essays, which, if I can make such a claim, are doing their best to make some sense. As for the selection of nonsense, it is embraced here in the widest sense: there is the pure nonsense of 'Impossibilia' – a genre that exclusively handles the untrue and inconceivable – as well as that of phonetic poems consisting of words that are devoid of meaning. But there is also the ample territory where sense and nonsense become entangled. After all, reality doesn't have to be excluded as long as it is altered, contradicted or compromised. Such texts tend to be comical unless they are written by the mentally ill. Sense and nonsense combined – does it not represent the true condition of man? We can also spell it out paradoxically in Paul Valéry's words: 'Two dangers threaten the world: sense and nonsense.'

For Immanuel Kant, both music and laughter belonged to the realm of nonsense. One doesn't 'think of anything' yet remains able to be 'vividly entertained'. (The possibility of thinking in purely musical terms seems to have eluded him.) Delightfully, he calls genius dependent on whim (*Laune*), for whim 'has spirit' (*Geist*) while order doesn't.*

My selection of nonsense texts covers the whole gamut from 'poetic' to the 'anti-poetic'. It makes do without Carroll and Lear who are sufficiently known, as well as without Hugo Ball's *Karawane* or Kurt Schwitters's *Ursonate*, canonic texts that were amply resurrected during the Dada centenary of 2016. Christian Morgenstern's 'Das Knie' remains the quintessential German nonsense poem. Charles Amberg's 'Tearing Out One of His Eyelashes', on the other hand, is the Dada cabaret song par excellence. Let me start with Daniil Kharms.

* Kant, *Reflexionen zur Anthropologie*, 802 und 922.

Daniil Kharms

translated by Alfred Brendel

THERE WAS A MAN

There was a man.

He owned a nose.

So he owned a nose that looked like a mouth.

So he owned a nose that looked like a mouth
with two ears.

VI

Pushkin loved to throw stones. Wherever he saw stones he'd start throwing them.

Sometimes he would warm to his task, standing there, crimson-faced, waving his arms, throwing stones – simply appalling.

VII

Pushkin had four sons, and all were idiots. One of them couldn't even sit on a chair without constantly falling off. But even Pushkin himself had trouble sitting on a chair. As it frequently happened – what a hoot! – they were all sitting at the table. At one end, Pushkin fell off his chair, at the other end, his son. Quite intolerable.

THE INVENTOR ANTON PAVLOVIČ ŠILOV

The inventor Anton Pavlovič Šilov sat down on a little bench in the Summer Garden (there is, in St Petersburg, a garden that bears this name, and the incident that I shall now describe occurred in the winter of 1933.)

'All right,' said Anton Pavlovič. 'Let's assume the lever is correctly attached and propels the bomb upwards.'

Everything and Nothing: Dada 2016

As Switzerland was neutral during the First World War, Zurich became a refuge for artists, writers, intellectuals, pacifists, and young men of various nationalities avoiding conscription. In 1916 several of them decided to create a new kind of evening entertainment. They called it Cabaret Voltaire and established it at No. 1 Spiegelgasse, not far from the room occupied by an occasional visitor to the cabaret, Vladimir Ilich Lenin.

The group, which became known as Dadaists, consisted of two Germans (Hugo Ball and Richard Huelsenbeck), one Alsatian (Hans Arp) and two Romanians (Marcel Janco and Tristan Tzara), and was complemented by two women, the German Emmy Hennings and the Swiss Sophie Taeuber. They were soon joined by the Czech national Walter Serner. The youngest, Tzara, was twenty; Hennings, the oldest, thirty-one. All were united in their loathing of the war.

The initiator of the group appears to have been Hugo Ball. He was, like the majority of Dadaists, a writer but he had also worked for theatre and cabaret. As a pacifist he had had to leave Germany. Pale, tall, gaunt and near-starving, he settled with Emmy Hennings in Zurich, and was regarded as a dangerous foreigner. At the Voltaire, he declaimed his groundbreaking phonetic poem *Karawane* (Caravan) to the bemusement of the public. After a few intense months of Dada activity he parted company, turned to a gnostic Catholicism and died in the Swiss countryside, regarded as a kind of saint. His diary, *Die Flucht aus der Zeit* (The Flight from Time), remains one of the key accounts of Dadaism.

For Richard Huelsenbeck, noise, according to Hans Richter, seems to have been the most natural form of virility. Within Dada, he was the champion of provocation. A poet and journalist who subsequently travelled the world as a ship's doctor and practised for a time in New York as a psychoanalyst, Huelsenbeck persevered with Dada and helped to establish its markedly different Berlin branch.

Among the artists of stature emerging from Dada, Hans Arp was perhaps the steadiest and most consistent. A friend of Max Ernst, Schwitters and Wassily Kandinsky, and a gifted poet, he was considered to be the most balanced member of the group, devoid of malice and envy, and endowed with a superior sense of humour. Sophie Taeuber, who was later to marry Arp, was a notable artist herself, teaching at the Applied Arts School in Zurich. She created marionettes, and was a member of Rudolf von Laban's dancing school, which had established a new expressive style of dance. During her Dada appearances as a dancer, she had to wear a mask to disguise her identity.

In Tristan Tzara, calm and self-assured yet endowed with a thunderous voice, Dadaism had its most passionate advocate and its most tireless propagandist. André Breton called him a charlatan hungry for fame but was reconciled with him in 1929. Tzara's poems influenced Allen Ginsberg and William Burroughs, and a few of them were translated by Samuel Beckett. Like Arp, he subsequently became a Surrealist. Tzara's fellow Romanian Marcel Janco was described as a handsome melancholic, a ladies' man who played the accordion and sang Romanian songs. He was a painter and sculptor who was to become a leading architect in Bucharest and Israel. He created masks for the Zurich Dadaists, and spoke, or rather shouted, simultaneous poems alongside Tzara and Huelsenbeck.

Emmy Hennings, before living with Hugo Ball, had been an alluring drifter. *Diseuse*, actress, barmaid and model, she became the femme fatale for more than a few German poets. She was a gifted cabaret artiste who sang 'Hab keinen Charakter, hab nur Hunger' ('Devoid of character, I'm just hungry'). She was an important presence at the Dada events, and 'her couplets', according to Huelsenbeck, 'saved our life'.

Soon, there was also Walter Serner, a Dada outsider, cynic and anarchist who, as a writer, would become notorious for his thrillers and scandalous novels. This was a time when dandies wore monocles. Serner did, and so did some of his Dadaist colleagues. He rebelled against society by being a high-class confidence trickster, producing a juridical thesis of which 80 per cent later turned out to be plagiarised. Under the name of his painter friend Christian Schad, he reviewed a collection of his own stories. He also enjoyed feeding the press false information. His essay 'Letzte Lockerung' (Ultimate Loosening) is, for some, a Dadaist classic.

From the near-improvisation of the initial events at the Cabaret Voltaire, one of the most influential avant-garde movements was to emerge. The word 'Dada' was first used only a couple of months later. There are several explanations for it: the babble of a child, the word for a toy, the double 'yes' in Slavic languages and Romanian, and a Dada lily-milk soap and hair tonic, which was first produced in 1912.

Dada was a joint achievement of the group. Its soirées were multimedia events: they combined words and litera-ture, singing, music (with Ball at the piano), dance, art, farce, and a fair amount of noise. 'Repelled by the butch-eries of the 1914–18 World War, we surrendered to the arts,' said Hans Arp. 'We looked for an elemental art that would free the people from the insanity of the times, and for a new order that might establish a balance between heaven and hell.' 'What we were celebrating', declared Hugo Ball, 'was a *buffonade* and a requiem at the same time.'

In spite of many utterances to the contrary, the striving of most Dadaists seems to have been directed towards a new art that would have nothing to do with former styles and notions. In order to find it, every novel means of expression was absorbed, if not invented: abstraction, photomontage, collage, assemblage, frottage, typography, glossolalia; phon-etic, concrete, visual and simultaneous poetry, conceptual art, the readymade, the drawing and painting of invented machines, happening, performance, and kinetic art, including film. No less crucial was the inspiration that came from three areas subsequently fundamental to most visual artists of the twentieth century: artefacts from Africa and Oceania that had been labelled 'primitive', the art of the insane, and the drawings of children.

There was an overwhelming need for the wild, the simple and the unreflective. While African masks and children's art were included in exhibitions at the Galerie Dada, there was a personal connection to Hans Huber, the owner and director of a mental hospital. He befriended Arp, Richter, Serner and others, liberally guiding his guests through his establishment and even housing some of them for weeks. Hans Richter, who later became one of the most sensible chroniclers of Dada,* tells us that while he and the poet Albert Ehrenstein were staying at the house, the presence of another house guest, the actress Elisabeth Bergner, a leading star of early film then scarcely twenty years old, provided the kind of thrill without which even the most hospitable psychiatrist 'wouldn't have been able to keep us there'.

Immediately after the war, Dada branches in Berlin, Paris, Cologne and Amsterdam sprang up. But I should mention that, before the official christening of Dada, an important New York group of pre-Dadaists had already

* Hans Richter, *Dada Profile* (Zurich, 1961).

been active. Hardly any other Dada objects have ever been as fervently discussed as the 'readymades' produced by the great Marcel Duchamp, while Francis Picabia excelled in the elegant depiction of machines that had no obvious purpose. Man Ray later emerged as the unsurpassed portrait photographer of the Parisian arts scene. In New York, there was also the French-born Edgard Varèse, one of the few musicians of future importance among early Dadaists. Musically, the Zurich group leaned towards the bruitism of the Futurist Luigi Russolo, and Huelsenbeck produced as much pandemonium as possible on his kettledrum. (Exceptionally, a composer called Hans Heusser was involved in the soirées a couple of times. He later became a notable provider of Swiss military marches.)

In Paris, Tzara created a stir with his *Manifeste Dada 1918* as well as with his subsequent electrifying presence. There, Erik Satie, another major composer, was a Dada sympathiser, and the literary ground had been prepared by the poet Guillaume Apollinaire. From 1920 on, Breton and a number of writers and artists who later became Surrealists joined Tzara. In 1922, the Dadaists officially fell out with one another, according to Theo van Doesburg, over the question of whether a locomotive was more modern than a bowler hat.

The profound difference between Dada and Surrealism was that the Surrealists had a programme and a leader (Breton) while Dada was freewheeling and steeped in ambiguity. It was everything as well as nothing. Neverthe-less, each of its branches had a different character. Berlin Dada, with Huelsenbeck, Raoul Hausmann and Johannes Baader – an eccentric who invaded the National Assembly to distribute Dada leaflets – was the most aggressive and political. The virtuoso draughtsman George Grosz despised bourgeois culture as well as modern art.

Man Ray, *Le Cadeau* (*The Gift*), *c.* 1958. New York, Museum of Modern Art (MoMA)

Hausmann, a Dadaist with philosophical ambitions, and his companion Hannah Höch became champions of photomontage and collage, techniques central to Dadaism. In Hanover, the unsurpassed master of collage turned out to be Kurt Schwitters, an artist of genius with a very different temperament: apolitical, and totally devoted to 'Merz', his own brand of Dada. An amazingly tall figure, he used his booming voice to declaim, shout, hiss and scream his mighty poem *Ursonate*, to this day the most striking specimen of phonetic poetry. His recitations were said to be so impressive that audiences were seized first by laughter, then by awe. Schwitters was also part of the Amsterdam Dada scene connected to Theo van Doesburg and the Constructivist movement De Stijl.

In Cologne, Max Ernst produced some of the most exquisite Dada drawings and photomontages of the early 1920s. Together with the son of a banker who called himself Baargeld (cash), he shocked his father and the Rhinelanders with a Dada exhibition that was promptly closed by the police. A Dada sentence by Max Ernst highly suitable for guestbooks reads: 'Nach uraltem, ängstlich behütetem Klostergeheimnis lernen selbst Greise mühelos Klavier spielen.'* Italian Dadaists included the poet Giuseppe Ungaretti, the painter Enrico Prampolini and the polymath Alberto Savinio. The fact that Dada soon enjoyed a near-global resonance was amply confirmed by the imposing Dada retrospective of 2005–6 at the Centre Pompidou in Paris that assembled a thousand works by fifty artists.

In the decade before the war, Cubism, Futurism, Expres-

---

* 'Thanks to an ancient, closely guarded monastic secret, even the aged can learn to play the piano with no trouble at all.' (My translation)

sionism and, in England, Vorticism had rocked the boat of aesthetics. Simultaneously, tonality and functional harmony that had worn thin in music were abolished by the more enterprising of composers. What Dada did a few years later was more radical. It turned against anything aesthetic, moral or intellectual, or relating to culture, ideology, religion or national identity, in order to create something out of nothing. Impressed by Friedrich Nietzsche and Henri Bergson, the Dadaists turned against the philosophy of Kant. Huelsenbeck's *Dada Almanach* of 1920 quotes Nietzsche's *Jenseits von Gut und Böse*:

> We are prepared . . . as no time has ever been, for a carnival in the grand style, for the most spiritual laughter and hijinks, for the transcendental heights of the highest nonsense (*Blödsinn*) and aristocratic derision of the world. Maybe what we shall discover right there is the empire of our *invention*, that empire where even we can still be originals, perhaps as parodists of world history and God's harlequins. Possibly, if nothing else from our day warrants any future, it is precisely our laughter that has future.

According to Schwitters, 'Dada subsumes all big tensions of our time under the biggest common denominator: Nonsense . . . Dada is the moral gravity of our time while the public collapses with laughter. As do the Dadaists.'

Kurt Schwitters, *Konstruktion für edle Frauen*
(*Construction for Noble Ladies*), 1919. Los Angeles
County Museum of Art (LACMA)

Kurt Schwitters, *Mz 334 Verbürgt rein*, 1921.
Marlborough Fine Art (London) Ltd

Dada relished contradictions. A famous Dada saying claimed that whoever is a Dadaist is against Dada. In his *Manifeste Dada 1918*, Tristan Tzara informs us that, as the editor, he wants to emphasise that he feels unable to endorse any of the opinions expressed since he was against mani- festos in principle. But also against principles. Theo van Doesburg called Dada the 'art form on account of which its producer doesn't take a stand for anything. This relative art form is accompanied by laughter.'

In his admirable book *Modernism – Dada – Postmodernism* Richard Sheppard explains:

> The word Dada is used at three levels. At the first level, it names an amorphous bohemian movement. At the second level it characterises a complex of existential attitudes, which, while varying from person to person, are vitalist and involve the achievement of balance amid fluctuating opposites. But at the third level, it is used by some of the Dadaists to name a life force that is simultaneously material, erotic and spiritual, creative and destructive.*

My particular sympathy goes to the second level. In my young years I envisaged a sphere within which all contradictions and opposites were contained in such a way that

* Richard Sheppard, *Modernism – Dada – Postmodernism* (Northwestern University Press, 2000), p. 197.

the centre of the sphere would be the meeting point of the centres of all the opposites – you could call it the ultimate nothingness, or God. To live with, and balance out, the contradictions seems a noble goal. It was as a child that I unwittingly encountered Dada in its funniest form. At home, my mother sang, to her own embarrassment, a Berlin cabaret song from the 1920s that starts with the memorable line 'I'll tear out one of my eyelashes and stab you dead with it', and ends with the intention to order a fried egg 'and sprinkle you with spinach'. It was much later that I realised that sense and nonsense need to be partners in order to mirror the absurdity of this world.

As for the third level, mysticism – Christian, Zen or Tao – had been crucial to Arp, Ball and Baader. The Dadaists of New York, Paris or Cologne, however, didn't have much use for it. Mysticism was within the reach of, but not central to, Dada. And where it was pursued it was often handled, in the Dadaist mode, with some irony.

It is strange that the comic side of Dada has been all but ignored by some commentators. This reminds me of the fact that at the bicentenary of Haydn's death in 2009 there were several tributes that didn't mention his musical sense of humour. The impressive catalogue of the Dada exhibition at Rolandseck, the place where Hans Arp spent his final years, includes a list of Dada-related topics: mysticism, psyche, philosophy, literature, art, language, soirée, Africa, mask, dance and revolt. Laughter is missing. Has there ever been a major avant-garde movement that was so closely tied to laughter and the grotesque? Laughter was the Dadaists' favourite instrument, a joint anarchic impulse. Aggressive, sarcastic, sardonic, it could also be, as in Arp's case, serene. By laughing, Dadaists protested against those who took laughter as an indecent aberration in the tradition of the Aprocryphal saying, 'A fool laughs overly loud; a wise man makes do with a faint smile' (Ecclesiasticus 21:20). Traditionalists see Dadaists as silly people. To a degree, they are right. Silliness was liberation from the constraints of reason. It has the potential to be funny, to provoke laughter, and make people realise that laughter is liberating. To Dadaists, Charlie Chaplin was the greatest artist of the world.

Two concepts, Carl Gustav Jung's 'Trickster' and Mikhail Bakhtin's 'Carnival', can help to illuminate Dada mores, mirth and poetry. The 'Trickster' is presented as a creature simultaneously sub- and superhuman while Bakhtin's 'Carnival' signifies 'an escape from humanly opposed, officially sanctioned norms'.* It generates 'cosmic humor' and juxtaposes opposites. Raoul Hausmann mentioned the sanctity of nonsense and 'the jubilation of Orphic absurdity'.

There is another view of laughter that might have saved the Dadaists from a more uncivilised sort of aggression.

* Sheppard, p. 292.

According to the sociologist Norbert Elias, whoever laughs doesn't bite.

Compared to Dada's achievement in the visual arts, its literary strengths have remained less evident. Major artists who started as Dadaists – Ernst, Schwitters, Arp, Duchamp, Man Ray, Picabia – have been exhibited worldwide, and Hannah Höch is belatedly identified as one of the finest female artists of her time. As most Dadaists were dual talents, one can find some verbal counterpoints in what they produced visually. The techniques of photomontage, collage and assemblage permeated some of their poetry as well: words were arranged at random, or used against their meaning, or employed as an abstract succession newly invented, a quasi-language that needed to be declaimed, and listened to. And to be seen as well, as long as typography was employed to enliven the visual impression of the page.

In the opening *Dada Manifesto* of 1916, Hugo Ball said that Dada poems aimed to dispense with a language that had been ravaged and had become unacceptable. In Arp's words, Dada poetry 'doesn't try to depict anything, nor does it interpret'. To Emmy Hennings, the poet Arp appeared to have come from another planet, 'most mysterious yet thoroughly acceptable'. While performing his poems he was said to have had a hold on the public similar to that of Grock, the great and deeply affecting clown, who needed only to utter two words, 'nicht möglich' ('impossible'), to enrapture the crowd.

Another literary genre, one that Dada shared with other movements of the time, is the manifesto. A large number of mostly short-lived periodicals helped make Dadaism known in many countries disseminating Ball's, Huelsenbeck's, Tzara's, Picabia's, Doesburg's and Schwitters's speeches, articles and buffooneries. One of the most comprehensive of these publications was Huelsenbeck's *Dada Almanach* of 1920. The picture on its cover follows the example of Duchamp's bearded *Mona Lisa* by depicting a mustachioed Beethoven.

In 2016, Zurich, better known for its commercial power than for its anarchic leanings, was celebrating a Dada season. In this jubilee year, the city exuded more than a whiff of carnivalesque excitement. The Zurich Festival, almost entirely dedicated to Dada, included three Dada soirées and a multitude of theatrical and academic events. Its crowning glory might well have been the performance of the Symphony for nine Harley-Davidsons, Trumpet and Synthesiser by the octogenarian avant-garde composer Dieter Schnebel. It was performed at the Münsterhof, a square in Zurich's inner city that had just been designated a traffic-free zone. The event included a hooting scherzo and a motorcycling ballet, and was conducted by Steffi Weismann, a woman in red overalls braving the rain. Another attractively Dadaesque venture was the organisation of dinner encounters in ten private houses. The paying guests were informed only in the afternoon where the dinner would take place. During the evening there would be surprise readings, literary experiments, music and improvisation. Guests were expected to participate.

Two exhibitions opened the season. The first, small but exquisite, was more than an exhibition: it offered a reconstruction of *Dadaglobe*, an anthology of international Dadaism the publication of which had been abruptly cancelled in 1921. A joint project by Tzara and Picabia, it had assembled a multitude of contributions that were relocated in recent years mainly thanks to the work of Adrian Sudhalter who, in the catalogue, enlightens her readers with a sharply perceptive account of the project's history. A rival enterprise called *Dadaco* had come to nothing due to a lack of funds. Reasons for the cancellations of *Dadaglobe*, on the other hand, have remained obscure. Possible causes were personal quarrels, Picabia's and Tzara's ill health, Picabia's noisy parting from Dada, and censorship that mistook the large influx of international letters and material for a political threat. The fact that the project was not mentioned again remains conspicuous.

The Kunsthaus Zürich did itself proud with a catalogue that assembles the complete remains of *Dadaglobe*. Within the quickly multiplying Dada literature it occupies a place of honour.

sittin on the Dina toilet

Dad

Eco!

Vlad

PAVLA

no hatschi

DADA? I am beautiful
- Dini Mone
n Twins ♡

no Who I am

was here ▼

you think your
weie here ! ....
mes ♡   Berlin

KIAN
JC

Pawla

Dada

DA   DA

lalolu ikt eü lalala
Hatila te vay arlilo

DADA !

1 1 2 3 5 8 13 2

Jo, jo, jo
Nei, nei, nei
doch, doch, doch
aber, aberaberal

Laura you are my
BFFE ♡

★ ☆ ✱ ✱ ☮ ♡ ⊘

5 72

... war, war Da...

KOREA 한국인 갇크리아
이용우 이탈리아 → 스위스
20대 배낭여행 대한민국 스위스
↓ 체 코
갇연최 깜디 ♡..

bei D
gibt es Ko
Sachen die z
lustig sind

Von ch

ich lasse ...
d Riss...
ich bin so kle...
wie eine Ma...
ihre so gro...
e ein Rau...

Make the World be...

DADA LAC

? ? ? ? ? ?
DaDa Movement
痕子+天才+
不滿+反戰
ART

mimmo 21...

TIM

...Dada

Jeda Monch

$\log a\Upsilon = \dfrac{\sin\alpha}{...} = \text{Peter}$ $\Delta T = V_0 \cdot \Delta V \cdot \Upsilon$

Dada ist die Postnukleare Nacht!
DON'T BE A MAYBE BE A DADA!
Dada für Gaga
DU PA DU SRA
moma
Man's worst enemy... Man himself
NEIN NO
DADA
ARCHITECTURE
BRANKO
DADABU GUTI
NOCH EIN DADA!
Es ist nicht alles Dada, aber vieles ist Gaga!
WOHIN GEHST DU
Marvin & Gianna
ist schön
AVOID SOCIAL MASS MEDIA
BANANE
DADA smoke
1'000 000 000 FRS
DADA SARA en BCN
HaHa Dada
Peace and Love
Dada
Prirlady
Dada lebt!! weiter
BISOLLOL
Dada BISOLINO
GISELA
nicht otto ola doch ja
420

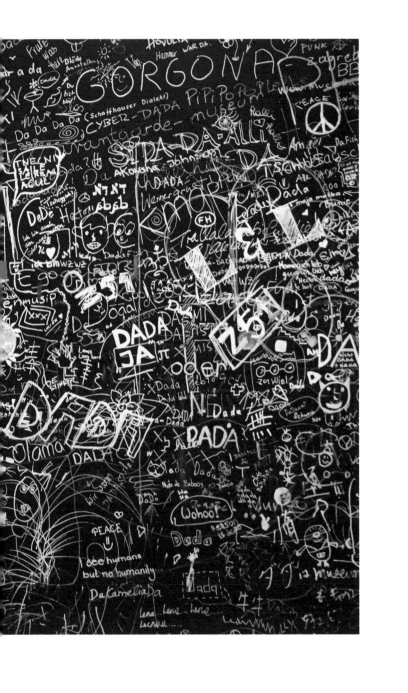

Dada Universal, graffiti. Landesmuseum Zürich, 2016

The second exhibition, which had no catalogue, was mounted in a large barn right next to the railway station. It belonged to the Landesmuseum Zürich and was, in true Dada fashion, demolished as soon as the exhibition closed. The premises were ideal. The interior was completely black. One of the shorter walls served as a kind of blackboard for visitors who were encouraged to provide graffiti with white chalk. By the last day of the exhibition, however, every inch of all the walls was magnificently covered with words or drawings. There was a constant presentation of films ranging from Hans Richter's abstract rectangles to Mary Wigman's *Witch's Dance*. In glass cases, Dada-related objects were displayed and juxtaposed. What the curators Stefan Zweifel and Juri Steiner accomplished was greatly appreciated by a predominantly young public but also, it seems, by a visiting group of psychoanalysts.

More exhibitions were to follow. The large and perplexing survey of Francis Picabia's work, also at the Kunsthaus, offered a complete overview of his deliberate strategy of irony and contradiction. André Breton, one of Picabia's staunchest allies, described it in his final tribute: 'An oeuvre based on the sovereignty of caprice, on the refusal to follow, entirely based on freedom, even to displease.' It was Picabia's tough luck that his contemporary Pablo Picasso gave an example of an artist remaining in command in spite of all his Protean changes of tack. Picabia didn't have, and didn't seem to want, an aesthetic self. Appropriately, he hated 'taste': 'My great fear is to be taken seriously, to become a great man, a master.' Which didn't prevent him from producing some striking works of art.

Even as a child he embodied the *enfant terrible*. By the time he was fifteen he had acquired a skill so brilliant that he copied his father's collection of Spanish paintings, replacing the originals with his reproductions. He then sold the originals to finance his stamp collection.

Not unlike Picasso, Picabia (1879–1953) was a craftsman of staggering virtuosity. Both liked to produce at great speed. With Picabia speed became, as he said, 'a wild desire', also indulged when driving automobiles, of which he seems to have owned 127. (Among artists affiliated with Dada, Picabia was the wealthiest by far.) The notion of movement and speed becomes apparent in his masterly abstract pictures of 1912–13. Here, as in the paintings of his close friend Marcel Duchamp, Cubism is being galvanised by the Futurist impetus of frenzied motion. The very large abstractions *La source* and *Edtaonisl* seem to me his supreme achievements. Inch by inch, they are full of invention, a term hardly applicable to his work in general, as he elsewhere preferred to use prefabricated shapes and images: picture postcards were turned into Impressionist and Pointillist canvases, technical drawings were wittily distorted, and photographs from girlie magazines were slickly presented as paintings. (In his later work, the urge to offend through kitsch reveals a mixture of cynicism and contempt.)

Hardly less astonishing is the following period, 1914–15, of 'Machinist' paintings and drawings, described by Picabia as a 'pinnacle of mechanical symbolism' – pre-Dada creations of a peculiar distinction that include words and titles linking them to some of his writings, including *Unique eunuque* and *La veuve joyeuse*. Mechanomorphs continued to figure deliciously in the nineteen issues of the magazine *391*, which Picabia masterminded.

I shall not dwell on the lowest point of Picabia's activity, the trashy paintings of the war years 1939–45, and remain grateful for the fact that within the minimum of nine – hugely varied – phases of his rollercoaster output there is hardly one that doesn't include a major work.

The comprehensive and sumptuous catalogue, assembled by Anne Umland of New York's MoMA and Cathérine Hug of the Kunsthaus Zürich, seems destined to remain the principal source of reference. Rachel Silveri's extensive and painstaking account of Picabia's life mentions his propensity for anti-Semitic and proto-Fascist remarks but also his verve in hosting vastly successful soirées, *fêtes* and galas at Cannes's Casino aux Ambassadeurs that could include monkeys and palm trees if not lions and panthers. Altogether, the amount of excellent female editors and enablers connected to Zurich's Dada enterprise deserves special attention.

The association of Zurich's Galerie Gmurzinska with the art of Kurt Schwitters dates back nearly five decades.

Francis Picabia, *Edtaonisl (Ecclesiastic)*, 1913.
The Art Institute of Chicago

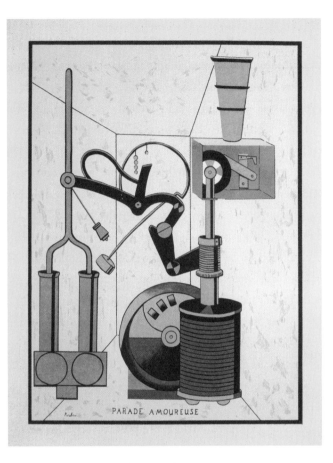

PARADE AMOUREUSE

Francis Picabia, *Parade amoureuse*, 1917.
Mr and Mrs Morton G. Neumann

At the very premises that had housed the short-lived Galerie Dada a century earlier, seventy of Schwitters's works were presented in a most unusual fashion. The late architect Zaha Hadid had turned the gallery space into a dreamscape of fluid forms that vividly demonstrated the hold Schwitters's *Merzbau*, his own architectural venture, had on her imagination. While Schwitters, with all his Dadaist leanings, remained an artist in pursuit of form and balance, his pictorial compositions also show a superlative control of colour. I remember the huge Schwitters exhibition in Paris in 1994 at the Centre Pompidou where, surrounded by collages, the viewer got the impression of being confronted by the rarefied palette of a painter. In Schwitters's work in his final years, humour and playful grace may have disappeared. It is harsher and gloomier but, as time has proved, hardly less distinguished.

Finally, in Zurich's splendid Museum Rietberg, Dada objects were exquisitely displayed next to specimens of African sculpture. (In 1915, Carl Einstein had been the first to refer to 'primitive' African sculpture as art.) The juxtaposition had a revelatory effect. To see Hannah Höch's spellbinding collages *Aus einem ethnographischen Museum* (*From an Ethnographical Museum*) in such a context was a moving experience. In Berlin, this exhibition was shown in a larger format in autumn 2016.

*

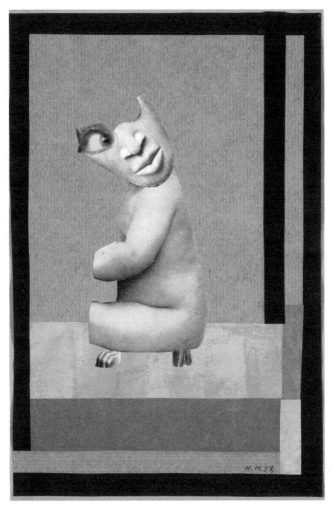

Hannah Höch, *Aus der Sammlung: Aus einem ethnographischen Museum* (*From the Collection: From an Ethnographic Museum*). Edinburgh, Scottish National Gallery of Modern Art

Dada was not a fashion, a style or a doctrine. It was more than a footnote to cultural history. We can better understand it as a condition, a spirit, a productive state of mind that has remained alive. Looking for core elements within the chaotic non-structure of Dada, I would mention paradox, chance, abandon, protest, aggression, anti-nationalism, humour, irony, bluff, art and mysticism. To be sure, art has been attacked and derided by a number of Dadaists. Yet the most impressive results of its activities seem to me to belong to the visual arts, while, for a majority of Dadaists, mysticism doesn't appear to have been an issue. Neither was political engagement, a peculiarity of Berlin Dada. Depending on the composition of ingredients, different types of Dadaists emerged. But there is also the distinction between relentless, full-time Dadaists such as Tzara and those for whom Dada was a necessary complement. Hans Richter said that the desire for anarchy, chaos and surrender to chance *and* the desire for order had governed his life since at least 1917.* I would readily list myself among those to whom the dance amid contradictions constitutes an essence of life.

In most of the post-1945 art movements, I can see traces of Dada. There are links to the happenings of Fluxus during the 1960s, to the Stuttgart group of Max Bense and various other units of concrete poetry, to Vienna's Aktionismus, to

* Sheppard, p. 189.

Monty Python, and to punk. (A punk rock band even called itself Cabaret Voltaire.) On my personal list of honorary Dadaists I wouldn't like to miss the name of Jean Tinguely, the sculptor both funny and cosmic (in his *Metamachines*). The self-destruction in 1960 of his interconnected objects in the garden of New York's MoMA was a quintessential Dada event. I should further mention Gary Larson's cartoons, Philip Guston's late cartoons and paintings, some of Mauricio Kagel's later compositions (*10 Marches to Miss the Victory*), and György Ligeti's *Aventures et Nouvelles aventures*, a ravishing modern glossolalia, as well as his opera *Le Grand Macabre*. Not to forget Virgil Thomson's Piano Sonata for Gertrude Stein in three movements on four pages, all on white keys. Greetings also to James Joyce, a Zurich contemporary of the Dadaists, and to Daniil Kharms of the Oberiu group in Leningrad.

There seems to me more than a little resemblance between the world a hundred years ago and our present frame of mind. Mercifully, our world is not, at this moment, consumed by an all-out war. But it has plunged into a deep crisis. There is an overbearing feeling of menace, of being faced with a number of threats of supreme magnitude: the changing climate, atomic weapons, cyber criminality, terrorism, nationalism, demagoguery, overpopulation, xenophobia. Karl Kraus, Viennese moralist, satirist and critic, put it in a nutshell: 'Das Chaos sei willkommen, denn die Ordnung hat versagt' ('As order has failed, let chaos be welcome'). The buzz that Dada can generate these days in Zurich is best illustrated by the following. In February 2016, the Kunsthaus invited the people of Zurich to attend a fancy-dress ball coinciding with the *Dadaglobe* exposition. No fewer than nine hundred disguised Neodadaists turned up.

Velimir Khlebnikov

translated by Paul Schmidt

Hlahla! Uthlofan, lauflings!

Hlahla! Ufhlofan, lauflings!

Who lawghen with lafe, who hlaehen lewchly,

Hlahla! Ufhlofan hlouly!

Hlahla! Hloufish lauflings lafe uf beloght

lauchalorum!

Hlahla! Loufenish lauflings lafe, hlohan utlaufly!

Lawfen, lawfen,

Hloh, hlouh, hlou! luifekin, luifekin,

Hlofeningum, hlofeningum,

Hlahla! Uthlofan, lauflings!

Hlahla! Ufhlofan, lauflings!

INCANTATION BY LAUGHTER

translated by Vladimir Markov

O you laughniks, laugh it out!
O you laughniks, laugh it forth!
You who laugh it up and down,
Laugh along so laughily;
Laugh it off belaughingly!
Laughters of the laughing laughniks, overlaugh the
  laugherthons!
Laughiness of the laughish laughers, counterlaugh
  the Laughdom's Laughs!
Laughio! Laughio!
Dislaugh, relaugh, laughlets, laughlets,
Laughulets, laughulets,
O you laughniks, laugh it out!
O you laughniks, laugh it forth!

The Lady from Arezzo

On its main street, the Corso Italia, this Tuscan town offers a most spectacular view, that of the Chiesa Santa Maria della Pieve. Stepping out of the church through one of its Romanesque arcades, I spotted her on the other side of the street. She dwelt in a shop window now connected to a private art collection – not one of the mannequins that used to be part of a painter's studio's inventory but a specimen of the Baroque era manufactured to display women's attire while nevertheless retaining the features of a Piero della Francesca Madonna. After all, the place where this happened to me was Arezzo, where Piero created his sublime cycle of murals in the Church of San Francesco.

There are portraits whose eyes follow you everywhere. The Lady from Arezzo avoids you wherever you are. Without seeing the viewer, her eyes are open. Vividly, they gaze into her inner world, into the egg on top of her head. Below the waist, the creature makes do with a long-legged wooden frame, the abstractness of which lends her an eeriness worthy of Giorgio de Chirico. In its place, the shape of a female body would appear unimaginably profane. Nothing should imperil the dominance of the lady's head and its demonstration of Piero's nobility, notably that of his Marias who accept their impregnation in stoic innocence. In Piero's *Pala*

Montefeltro, the Virgin towers over six saints and four angels while one of the most notorious villains of the Quattrocento, Duke Federico, kneels in the foreground, presenting his broken nose. Hanging above the Madonna, an ostrich egg vouches for purity and divine perfection. Franco Fedeli, a local Arezzo artist well versed in dealing with historic dressmaker's dummies, applied the egg directly to the lady's head – an inspired idea, without which the figure would lose all its mystery.

Beside its nobility, the lady's face shows a considerable amount of freshness. But is she still unapproachable? The slight parting of the beautifully modelled lips, the barely visible hint of her teeth, seem to leave the sanctity of Piero's Madonnas behind. If I now speak of love, I shall begin with her lips.

Charles Amberg

ICH REISS MIR EINE WIMPER AUS

Ich reiß mir eine Wimper aus
und stech dich damit tot.
Dann nehm ich einen Lippenstift
und mal dich damit rot.

Und wenn du dann noch böse bist,
weiß ich nur einen Rat:
ich bestelle mir ein Spiegelei
und bespritz dich mit Spinat.

CABARET SONG

translated by Alfred Brendel

After tearing out one of my eyelashes
I'll stab you dead with it.
Whereupon I take a lipstick
and paint you red.

Should you, however, keep sulking,
I know what ought to be done:
I'll ask for some fried eggs
and sprinkle you with spinach.

Joseph Haydn's *Seven Last Words*

*On the occasion of a performance by
the Hagen Quartet*

This work is unlike any other. It relates to the last utterances of Jesus as handed down by the Bible. In 1786, the prebendary of the Church of Santa Cueva in Cadiz had commissioned seven slow instrumental movements, which, in dealing with these texts, should deepen the religious contemplation. The Brotherhood of the Holy Grotto met in a large subterranean cave that had been unearthed beneath the church. During the first performance of the work, the whole interior was covered in black. Paintings by renowned artists, Goya included, and a richly decorated altar turned this Capella de la Cueva into a house of God. Between the pieces of music, there were sermons. I shall not comment on the biblical texts but rather speak about Haydn, the revered musician, who took it on himself to compose this extraordinary work.

Is there, apart from Shostakovich's Fifteenth String Quartet, another multi-movement composition that consists exclusively of a succession of slow pieces? If we include the introduction (*Maestoso ed adagio*), there are eight. Contrary to the image of Haydn as the 'classicist who put the house of music into order' I see him rather as a grandmaster of risk and surprise, an inventor of musical forms such as the double variation, and a composer who introduced humour into instrumental music. His mixing of musical means that were supposed to serve either the sublime or the profane made his contemporaries cringe, or smile. Salieri complained about the 'mescolanza di tutti generi' ('confusion of genres') in Haydn's Masses.

Haydn, much more than Mozart and even Beethoven, was adventurous in the choice of keys and the way they appear next to one another. The key sequence within the *Seven Last Words* is astonishing: D minor, B flat major, C minor, E minor, F minor, A major, G minor, E flat major, and C minor. Lining up largos, graves, adagios and lentos, all in sonata form and yet presenting different characters without sacrificing inner unity – such an extraordinary challenge Haydn was unable to resist. At the end of the work, however, such almost static absorption in slowness is briefly contradicted by the turbulence of the concluding *terramoto* (earthquake).

Next to the *Andante*-composer Mozart, Haydn, in his slow movements, shines as the master of *Adagio*. A friendship of such warmth and generosity between two superlative but temperamentally different composers is unparalleled in the annals of music. Haydn, in his later years, was the biggest musical celebrity of his time. The nineteenth century then tended to relegate him to the second rank. More recently, steps have been made to correct this and emphasise his merits as the creator of the string quartet and the classical piano sonata, as groundbreaking symphonist and master of memorable Masses. To quote Goethe: 'We are once more reminded that Haydn is facing us not perhaps as an accomplished follower but as a genius of veritable originality who in form and substance rises above his time like a phoenix.'

Of course, Haydn was the master and initiator of musical humour. According to his biographer Georg August Griesinger, he had the knack 'of luring the listener into the highest degree of the comical by frivolous twists and turns of the seemingly serious'. Griesinger further reports that 'the theoreticians were screaming about music being demeaned by comic trifling', an attitude among serious-minded people that has remained alive to this day. At the same time, gravity, if not deepest grief, have always remained within reach.

Haydn's *Seven Last Words* swiftly became famous as an orchestral work, and soon also in the subsequent string quartet version that has remained the most familiar. The composer who was the first to reveal what string quartets were presented here his strangest and most unusual contribution to the genre. What Haydn aimed for was to create music that was worthy of the sacred texts to such a degree that it might, as he himself put it, 'kindle the deepest impression even in the soul of the most unexperienced'.

This places extraordinary demands not just on the performers but also on a listening public that must have related to religion, and religious music, differently during the composer's lifetime.

Haydn's musical mastery stretched from folk song to fugue. No one had fused fugues with string quartets and the variation form before. In Haydn's personality Rococo and Enlightenment, devotion and wit, are close neighbours. To quote Goethe once more:

> Our Haydn is a son of our region. Whatever his accomplishments, he achieves them without heat; who, after all, would enjoy being overheated? Temperament, sense, intelligence, humour, sweetness, power, and, ultimately, naivety and irony, those true hallmarks of genius, must be conceded to him with the utmost certitude.*

Mozart cautioned Haydn about travelling to London – after all, he couldn't even speak English. In actual fact, during his extensive stays in England not only was the musician appreciated but also the man. The royal family invited Haydn some forty times and enjoyed his singing of some of his own canzonettas after dinner. (As a boy in Vienna, he had been a member of the choir of St Stephen's.) Haydn's

* Both Goethe quotes are taken from *Theater und Schauspielkunst.* (*Haydn's 'Schöpfung'.*)

London notebooks testify to his lively mind and the multitude of his interests.

The *Seven Last Words* is fundamentally removed from such worldliness. Stripped of anything distracting, the movements are musical meditations trying to achieve a simplicity that communicates an essence of feeling and, by means of musical restatement and repetition, establishes a kind of mantra. It is the task of the players to unite intensity with utter unpretentiousness, *cantabile* with expressive eloquence. When this happens, which is rarely enough, we may be able to imagine why Haydn himself held this work in such high regard.

It was a remarkable decision by the Spanish gamba player and conductor Jordi Savall to invite José Saramago, the Portuguese writer and atheist, to be involved in the performance of the *Seven Last Words* in the Cadiz cave in 2006. Saramago's literary contributions to the occasion are titled *The Last Words of Man*. Here is an extract from his text dealing with the lament 'My God, why hast thou forsaken me?': 'Whoever has said that God is the silence of the universe, and man the scream that gives meaning to this silence, has spoken correctly.' For Saramago, Jesus emerged as just a man.

One of Haydn's contemporaries reacted to the 'Fourth Word of the Cross' in a kindred spirit. Jean Paul's novel *Siebenkäs* includes the visionary prose poem 'Rede des toten Christus vom Weltgebäude herab, daß kein Gott sei' ('The

Dead Christ Proclaims that there is no God'). I quote from the translation by Alexander Ewing:

> And at this point a lofty, noble form, bearing the impress of eternal sorrow, came sinking down towards our group, and rested on the altar; whereupon all the dead cried out, 'Christ! Is there no God?' He answered, 'There is none.' . . . How every soul in this great corpse-trench of an universe is utterly alone? I am alone – none by me – O Father, Father! where is that boundless breast of thine, that I may rest upon it? . . . And I fell down and peered into the shining mass of worlds, and beheld the coils of the great serpent of eternity all twined about those worlds; these mighty coils began to writhe and rise, and then again they tightened and contracted, folding round the universe twice as closely as before; they wound about all nature in thousandfolds, and crashed the worlds together, and crushed down the boundless temple to a little churchyard chapel. And all grew narrow, and dark, and terrible. And then a great immeasurable bell began to swing in act to toll the last hour of Time, and shatter the fabric of the universe to countless atoms . . .

Here ends Jean Paul's nightmare.

Music: Light and Darkness

'Let there be light. And there was light.' The tremendous C major chord in Haydn's *Creation*, which overwhelms the listener after the 'desolate and obscure' musical introduction, remains one of the most stunning illuminations in all music. Here, as in Mozart's 'Jupiter' Symphony, Schubert's 'Great C major' Symphony and *Wanderer Fantasy*, Beethoven's *Diabelli Variations* or Schumann's *Fantasie*, Op. 17, the key of C major stands for light and brightness. As it happens, it consists, on the piano, of white keys only.

In Beethoven's Fifth Symphony, the triumphant emergence of C major in the finale has the power of a personal liberation while the *prestissimo* coda of the 'Waldstein' Sonata scythes down any possible doubt. The conquest of darkness generates a euphoria that rids us, for the time being, of all that is Saturnian.

In the *Adagio* of Beethoven's Op. 111 the key of C major redeems us in a profoundly different way. After the strife (*con brio ed appassionato*) of the first movement, the following *Arietta* transports us into a realm of calm and elation. Just once within the variation movement does the music leave C major: a trill gradually ascends to E flat before it leads, step by step, back to the recapitulation of the theme. Here we seem to have come closer to a mystical experience than in any other piece of music I know.

Musical light and darkness corresponded, for a time, to major and minor. In Schubert, the kinship became so close that it leads into a kind of musical chiaroscuro, if not into explosive tension, as in the G major String Quartet.

In Beethoven's late music, the use of the diminished seventh chord in passing harmonies is already starting to cloud the musical waters.

Beethoven: *Diabelli Variations*, variation 3, bars 20–24

The mysterious four bars that persevere on the diminished seventh chord introduce us to a harmonic sphere quite alien to Diabelli's waltz. More and more composers of the nineteenth century succumbed to the lure of this harmonically exterritorial chord, which, applied with moderation, enabled them to express the ominous and disconcerting. On the other hand, the effect of chromaticism, already so significant in Gesualdo, Bach and Mozart, continued progressively to undermine the solidity of functional harmony. Tonality and diatonic harmony became porous, and started to disintegrate. In the early twentieth century, some of the most enterprising composers drew the necessary conclusions: works such as Schoenberg's Op. 11 or Busoni's *Sonatina seconda* inaugurated the new, 'atonal' phase. Where traditional triads crop up in later music, as in Messiaen's *Turangalîla- Symphonie,* they can sound, to my ears, almost obscene.

There are composers who wrote predominantly in major keys. Among Mozart's many symphonies, piano concertos and piano sonatas, there are just a couple of minor-key works in each genre. Next to the splendour, warmth, gracefulness and classical completeness of Mozart's major-key music, the 'minor-key' Mozart strikes me as fundamentally different. His C minor is not defiant or heroic as in Beethoven; it seems rather to represent the superior power of fate. Here are the demons that, in Mozart, Busoni didn't care to acknowledge. In his piano music in particular, in pieces that appeared to be written for himself, such as the A minor *Rondo* and B minor *Adagio*, both C minor *Fantasies* and both minor-key sonatas, a private and solitary Mozart comes to the fore.

The contrast of major and minor had become particularly evident since Haydn's great C minor Sonata, if not before: slow movements in the major are now the focus of light in minor-key works such as Mozart's K. 466 and K. 491, while those in the minor provide concertos including K. 271, K. 482 or K. 488 with a melancholy, grave, if not tragic core. In Beethoven we may even find works in which the outer movements keep exclusively to the minor while the middle movement never leaves the major. I am thinking of two of his most famous sonatas: Op. 27 No. 2 and Op. 31 No. 2.

Although in much music of our time the notion of major and minor seems as remote as a mythical planetary system, our emotional reactions to it have remained alive. Even today we would scarcely perform a gavotte at a funeral or dance behind a cortège. Some of us have also learned to listen to post-tonal music with discriminating ears. But light and darkness can be suggested in various ways. Within the tonal range, we receive signals from the lowest to the highest, from the obscurity of the bass to the blinding brightness of the treble. György Ligeti, in his *Études*, presented breathtaking ascents and descents covering the whole keyboard. One might, in such a context, speak of brightly lit minor where it occurs in the treble, and dark major in the lower register. Chopin, in his *Préludes* in F minor and D flat major, gives us a juxtaposition of nocturnal uproar and luminous *cantabile*. As for the piano's bass register, it was Liszt who unleashed its full might. In *Funérailles* and *Sunt lacrimae rerum* there are sounds in the lowest register the shattering blackness of which had not been experienced before. *Sunt lacrimae rerum*, after all, is more than a lament about the failure of the Hungarian Liberation Wars 1848–9. Liszt dedicated the work to Hans von Bülow in 1872. In the same year, he visited Bayreuth and told Wagner and Cosima that they were responsible for Bülow's devastated frame of mind.

When we describe the sound of a pianist as being bright or dark, transparent or opaque, we are talking about the balances the player himself produces on the instrument. A too heavy bass line prevents the upper register from radiating. If the sound is bottom heavy it will be unable to float. Here, the mental concept that gives the bass as much prominence as the melody is partly to blame. A number of atmospheric possibilities connected to the pedal can be realised only when the balance favours the higher frequencies. In the *Rondo* of the 'Waldstein' Sonata we are high up on a mountain looking into the delicate haze (*pianissimo dolce*) and listening to a mountain song, a *chant montagnard*. Here the pedal is supposed to remain active over prolonged stretches. In the valleys, by contrast, there is dancing (*quasi senza pedale*) to Russian-flavoured tunes.

Tone painting undoubtedly exists, whereas the claim that the visual arts can strike us as 'musical' seems to be mere conjecture. 'The air was pierced by fiery lightning' has been set to music in Haydn's *Creation*, where we can also listen to 'the light flaky snow' and 'the effervescence of the turbulent sea'. 'The waters are swelled by the swarming fish', while the ground is burdened by the weight of animals – a weight musically portrayed by one sustained *forte* note of bassoon and contrabassoon. But Haydn was selective in what he entrusted to music: 'And God created the big whales' is left to a recitative.

Bright, dark, light, shade, colour, timbre, near, far – such visual terms have been readily adopted in musical discourse. Since music doesn't directly relate to the outside world, metaphor and analogy have to assist. Pianists are able to control, in their playing, simultaneously a number of musical distances and timbres, and the notion of foreground and background has become useful even to musical analysis. In the variation movement of Op. 111, subterranean and stratospheric sounds alternate. The word 'composition' belongs as much to music as to the fine arts. Let me also mention those special minds that hear various keys synaesthetically as clearly defined colours. The question is whether perceiving D major as orange or A flat minor as purple will greatly enhance the comprehension of the works.

In comparison, the use of vocabulary from the musical sphere in the visual arts is sparse. Some canvases can strike us as noisy or blatant, in utter contrast to a painter such as Giorgio Morandi, whose works induce complete silence – still lifes in the strictest sense of the word. Where a painting is praised as a symphony of colour, kitsch may be looming around the corner.

'Through night to light' – this is another concept music is able to illuminate. (Beethoven's *Fidelio* is a prime example.) It is grounded in the need to overcome chaos with the help of reason. But it also lives by the idea of good and evil. Light and darkness depend on one another. The darkness of lower registers can also suggest inwardness. Beethoven, in his 'Waldstein' Sonata, initially conceived an extensive *Andante* in F major as its middle movement. In its graceful charm, it barely moves away from the outside world: good reason to replace it by the profound *Introduzione* to the finale that is familiar to us today – a striking contrast to the extrovert nature of the outer movements. A glimpse into fathomless profundity is presented by variation 20 of the Diabelli set:

Beethoven: *Diabelli Variations*, variation 20, opening bars

At midpoint within the overall C major turbulence of the work, it discloses a primordial riddle that defies any solution.

Schubert's *Winterreise*

Ian Bostridge: *Schubert's Winter Journey: Anatomy of an Obsession* (Faber & Faber, 2015)

Among musical compositions of the highest order connected with the figure 24, the songs of *Winterreise* occupy a special place. They do not relate to the complete set of 24 major and minor keys, as do Bach's preludes and fugues of *Das wohltemperierte Klavier* or Chopin's *Préludes*. Schubert's *Winterreise* embraces twice a dozen songs that do not offer a kaleidoscope of diverse musical characters and conditions but maintain a continuous state of mind. They do not constitute a process, a narrative like their cyclical predecessor *Die schöne Müllerin*, but dwell in a kind of desperate stasis that horrified Schubert's friends. The fact that Wilhelm Müller's poems do not strive to be romantically enchanting earned them Heinrich Heine's approval.

When Schubert was born, Vienna was the musical capital of Europe. Of the three composers who earned the city its pre-eminence, Mozart was dead, Haydn had more or less retired, and only Beethoven was still active until very nearly the end of Schubert's short life. Living in the same city but hardly, if at all, being in touch, both wrote their amazingly audacious final chamber music works virtually next door to one another, and independently of each other, within a period of little more than three years. In 1827, the year Beethoven died, Schubert had started composing *Winterreise*, his supreme song-cycle.

After the deaths of Schubert's favourite singers, Johann Michael Vogl and Karl Freiherr von Schönstein, there was hardly a Viennese Schubert tradition to speak of. With the exception of Brahms, who resided in Vienna, and the Hellmesberger Quartet, all other major musicians who championed Schubert's music were passing visitors from abroad. Similarly, few of the renowned singers, conductors and pianists have been, or are, Austrian. In his enthralling book on *Winterreise* Ian Bostridge writes that Schubert's music 'was played by most of the great instrumentalists of the day'. There, for once, Bostridge is mistaken. Besides the Schuppanzigh Quartet, which premiered his String Quartet in A minor – and rejected *Death and the Maiden* telling Schubert to stick to composing songs in the future – I can think of only Karl Maria von Bocklet, whom Chopin called one of the best pianists in Vienna.

In the years before the First World War, Schubert became popular as a kitsch figure, triggered by Rudolf Hans Bartsch's novel *Schwammerl* and reinforced by the gruesome *Lilac Time*. Today mercifully forgotten, this operetta ruined Schubert's image for decades, dragging the composer into an abyss of bad taste. In the film, Schubert was embodied by the famous tenor Richard Tauber, who had started off as an esteemed Mozart singer.

After the Second World War, there followed a radical reaction: now Schubert had to be relentlessly depressive and, on top of that, homosexual. It helps to remember that Schubert (literally up to his death – *Der Hirt auf dem Felsen* is one of his very last compositions) was able to write happy and radiant music. As Bostridge aptly remarks, 'It is undoubtedly true that there is no clear and prescriptive relationship between life and art or art and life. To put it at its most crass, Schubert wrote jolly music when he was gloomy, and gloomy music when he was jolly.'

Who is the figure *Winterreise* very indistinctly presents? A pathological case? (Bostridge speaks of 'the madness of the wanderer'.) A hysteric? A depressive? To me, he seems to be an alienated melancholic, Romantic–Biedermeierish in the wake of Byron and of Goethe's Werther, and beset by post-Napoleonic political frustration. Not a madman but 'teetering on the edge of unreason' as Bostridge calls it in his comment on 'Der Leiermann'.

The absurd, the comical in *Winterreise* should, in Bostridge's view, never be resisted. In 'Der Greise Kopf' he even finds a 'laughing' triplet figure. There is certainly irony in Müller's poems. Wilhelm Müller was a poet whom Heine admired; he translated Marlowe into German, and died, little older than Schubert, in 1827. Reading his poems aloud there are passages where the irony is obvious, and can be spoken very differently from the way Schubert composed them. I can readily see *Winterreise* in connection with Beckettian absurdity. But is it in Schubert's music? What I would dispute is that *Winterreise* is ever comical. It's the only thing Schubert's music is not. He belonged for a while to a Viennese club called the Unsinnsgesellschaft (Nonsense Society) but his compositions do not betray this at all.

Schubert's close connection with literature was supported by his friends and admirers: poets, composers, painters, amateurs and state officials who frequently met to recite Goethe and discuss the latest published poetry. The fusion of words and music that Schubert achieved was not merely a result of his unique melodic gifts. His interpretation of the poems extended to the piano part, a novel and comprehensive way of revealing atmosphere, psychology and the words' poetic layers. On the piano, suddenly anything could be expressed. The introduction of each song presents the basic mood or even crystallises several strands of a poem. The prelude of 'Im Dorfe' famously compresses barking, rattling and snoring in one brief idea, while that of 'Der Lindenbaum' combines the murmur of the well, the rustling of the linden tree, and the sweetness of dreams. Since Schubert, it has become impossible to separate the singing line from the accompaniment. And since Dietrich Fischer-Dieskau, who did more than anyone else to bring Schubert's *Lieder* to international attention, the accompanist has mutated into a partner. In his thirty recorded performances of *Winterreise* several of his piano partners are soloists.

With *Schubert's Winter Journey: Anatomy of an Obsession*, Ian Bostridge proves to be one of the most compelling writers among musical performers, an author as erudite and vivid as he is entertaining. In his words: 'Living a piece as complex and resonant as *Winterreise* means engaging with it in all sorts of ways: understanding what it might mean for us now, as a message in a bottle set afloat in the cultural ocean of 1828. How does it relate to our concerns? How does it connect with us, however unexpectedly?' Bostridge provides answers rich in associations and fascinating digressions, and presents veritable little seminars on topics that often gain a surprising relevance to the understanding of text and score. There is an influx of various disciplines: history and natural history, physics, literature and psychology, to mention only a few, generate a wealth of detailed information communicated with a rare immediacy on the borderline between good speaking and good writing. What I miss in this multifaceted volume is an index.

As a rule, each song is adorned with a specific essay. 'Die Wetterfahne' informs us about marriage contracts in Metternich's time; 'Der Lindenbaum' brings in Thomas Mann's *Magic Mountain*; 'Auf dem Flusse' provides an exploration of ice, and the political ice age of Metternich; 'Rast' muses about black and white, police and censorship and the relationship between art and form; 'Einsamkeit' connects, in one of the finest chapters, Byron, Caspar David Friedrich, Jean-Jacques Rousseau and Wilhelm Müller; 'Der greise

Kopf' exploits 'Beckettian resonances'; 'Der Wegweiser' informs us with admirable lucidity about Schubert's failing health; 'Das Wirtshaus' deals with Schubert and religion; and 'Die Nebensonnen' surprises us with an explanation of phantom suns. On the way, in a piece on tears and crying, we learn that 'the tears shed in emotion contain 20–25 per cent more protein than those produced when chopping onions'. For the final song, 'Der Leiermann', Bostridge invokes Bob Dylan: 'It's not a million miles from his jingle-jangle to Schubert's hurdy-gurdy.' Yes, but let's settle for a few thousand. If this is a song that should be rather spoken than sung artists such as Lotte Lehmann and Peter Anders, who recorded *Winterreise* in the 1940s, could teach many a singer today how to speak.

Bostridge's *Winter Journey* is destined to reach a wider audience. It refrains from musicological jargon, explains technical terms and translates any foreign-language quote. To the musical and literary privilege comes Bostridge's visual sense. The book is greatly enhanced by the discerning choice of its illustrations. Never has the juxtaposition of Schubert and Caspar David Friedrich seemed more pertinent. The inclusion of George de la Tour's *Hurdy-Gurdy Player* is as inspired as, on the witty side, that of Dürer's *Six Studies of Pillows* in connection with 'Im Dorfe' (where pillows are mentioned just once), as well as the depiction of the nine positions of waltzing that illuminates 'Täuschung' ('a light dances in front of me'). We also savour the contemporary information that 'ten to eleven thousand deaths occurred annually in Vienna. The cause of death for about one fourth of these is consumption which can be brought on by immoderate waltzing' – a matter of ballroom dust damaging the lungs.

There is, however, one matter about which I heartily disagree. In his chapter on 'Wasserflut', Bostridge's focus is on the rhythm of this song, for once depriving the reader of fascinating ruminations on the psychological roots of fatigue or the physiological causes of limping. The bone of contention is triplet assimilation: should, in Schubert, the semiquaver following a dotted quaver be played simultaneously with the third triplet note as a 'dotted triplet'? And should the printed page reproduce Schubert's way of writing faithfully and place the semiquaver under or above the last triplet note, and not after it as printers conventionally do? In a song that is pervaded by such rhythms, and not only there, these are crucial questions. Bostridge pleads for polyrhythm, while I insist on assimilation. (I am most grateful for the utterly civilised way in which Bostridge conducts this argument.)

As I see it, this issue is a matter not of opinion or taste but of fact. Both the autograph and the first print, which Schubert corrected, make it very clear that assimilation is called for. No composer in a sane mind would have written down the final semiquaver of the right hand in bars 3, 17 and 45 as Schubert did if polyrhythm was intended; he would have written the note after the chord. (In Bostridge's book, regrettably, only the first bar of the autograph is reproduced.) Here is the first print, which follows the notation of the autograph:

Schubert: *Winterreise*, 'Wasserflut', opening bars

Why has this question resulted in so much confusion? Part of the blame lies with the printed editions. Max Friedländer's creditable one, probably the most frequently used for a long time, prints the semiquaver after the triplet. Even the edition graced with Fischer-Dieskau's name, while trying to be accurate and generally having semiquavers underneath the last triplet note, misplaces the last semiquaver of bar 3. And the new Bärenreiter edition perpetuates the misleading visual picture, though it rightly mentions in a footnote that, as the sources suggest, adjustment of the rhythm is advisable. Rhythm is also a visual matter: the notation should help the player to grasp it at once with his eyes.

Gerald Moore, the celebrated accompanist, had stated categorically that the rhythm of 'Wasserflut' 'should be played as it looks on the score'. The question is: on which score? If it is the manuscript and the first print that are consulted I am delighted to agree. Unfortunately these sources have for a long time hardly been considered. Among the performers of the past, Julius Patzak with Jörg Demus, Peter Schreier with Sviatoslav Richter, and Peter Pears with Benjamin Britten are the conscientious exceptions; on their recordings they render the rhythm properly, as did Fischer-Dieskau and Matthias Goerne in all the performances I shared with them.

But there is, besides the philological evidence, a further reason for disagreement. The musical result of adjustment sounds to me much superior to the fanciful notion of the 'dragging effect given verisimilitude to the picture of the tired wanderer half-blinded by tears' (Gerald Moore). Here, as in several other instances of Schubert's music, the simpler rhythmic solution is the natural, and Schubertian, one.

'And what about Beethoven?' some musicians will ask. Look at his so-called 'Moonlight' Sonata: surely, in its first movement, the upper voice should not be adjusted to the continuous triplet rhythm. No, indeed it shouldn't. But then, Beethoven applied a modern and literal notation while Schubert, another pupil of Salieri, still clung to practices derived from the Baroque, and not just in his triplet notation, but also in countless suspended notes, so-called appoggiaturas, that thankfully have been unravelled in Friedländer's edition. In his comments on the playing of Beethoven's piano works, the composer's pupil Czerny warns of adjustment in Op. 27 No. 2 – which suggests that it was still practised by many.

Now there may be those who say that one could decide to go against the letter for the purported gain of a rhythmical structure that sounds more adventurous. Bostridge writes, 'The score is of course more than a mere recipe, and it provides a necessary and containing discipline for performers, *something to kick against*.' I prefer to score a few Schubertian goals.

In defence of the unnamed critical listener who, during 'Wasserflut', irked Bostridge by turning to his neighbour, I should say that I, as a soloist, always avoided recognising fellow musicians in the audience. As a singer, I would probably have closed my eyes like Karajan, who conducted with eyes shut, and was famously asked by a member of the audience whether he needed a guide dog. However, I cannot but admire Bostridge's acuity, while trying to move his listeners, in managing to make out not only three different musicians but also the precise location where they were sitting (rows H and I).

It took a long time for cyclical works of music to be performed as an entity. Julius Stockhausen was the first to sing the whole of *Winterreise* in public in the 1850s, whereas Clara Schumann still left out pieces in Schumann's cyclical piano works or performed selected numbers from the song-cycles. Busoni may have been the first to present Chopin's *Préludes* and *Études* in their entirety. Today, we hear *Winterreise* complete and uninterrupted, unless singers such as Ian Bostridge decide to programme the first twelve songs only, a cycle in itself written and published before the dozen to follow.

I have heard *Winterreise* presented straightforwardly or whimsically, tragically or laconically, calmly or in a frenzy, old or young (the miller's apprentice in *Die schöne Müllerin* is definitely younger), poised or deranged, fast or very slow indeed (Richter with Schreier), sung by higher or lower voices male or female, offered in terms of *cantabile* singing or quasi-spoken. The fact is that Schubert, apart from a few rare dynamic indications, doesn't grant any markings to the singer – they are all to be found in the piano part. Slurs are written down only when a syllable is sung on more than one note. That means that the singer has to make a lot of decisions, instinctive decisions mostly, about how to let the notes follow each other, where to sing quasi-*legato*, and where to connect two notes by *portamento* (sliding up or down), a practice that can sound utterly natural if applied in the right places with the right conviction. (Listen to Lotte Lehmann.) He or she will also decide, whether consciously or unconsciously, how to sing long notes, how to colour the words with vowels open or closed, dark or luminous, and which consonants to stress for expression and distinctiveness. There are the prerequisites: a captivating quality of voice; the mastery and beauty of singing; the feeling for musical connections – from note to note, harmony to harmony, phrase to phrase; the range of feeling; the unity of words and music (never at the expense of the words); the plasticity of diction.

Among performers of *Winterreise*, the Austrian tenor Julius Patzak, who apparently never needed to have a singing lesson in his life, stands out in my memory not only because his was the first *Winterreise* I ever witnessed (in 1964, Patzak was sixty-six years old) but because he had an unforgettable way of giving colour to words such as 'Schnee': shining white. His 'Lindenbaum' was the most moving by being utterly simple.

Winterreise doesn't need updating, embellishing, transcribing or paraphrasing. There have been numerous attempts to film it or bring it on stage. I remember Peter Pears on TV tucked in a heavy winter coat and braving the snow, or another singer who was made to fly through the air like a crow. There has also been a performance on the viola in which the lack of words and their declamation made for a gaping void even for musical viewers who didn't know German. According to Bostridge, 'The imaginative space that a singer creates enhances the performance of song. The audience has no set-up props to engage with – only the music, the instrument, the bodies of the performers, the face of the singer.'

Ian Bostridge's book is brilliant and unique. But it is, of course, a book and not the performance. After reading it we may listen differently to one of the supreme works of art that, despite being tainted by death, makes life worth living.

Hans Arp

translated by Jeremy Adler

From CONSTELLATIONS

Enormous dragons drumming on the clouds
Enormous dragons drumming on the gates
Enormous dragons drumming on the mirrors
The dragons are wearing hats of kiddies' heads

The glassy heads are wearing iron hats
Magnetic nuts are growing on glassy sticks
The heads of glass are rolling from their pockets
Instead of heads the kids are wearing clouds

Ernst Jandl

translated by Jeremy Adler

MOUNTAIN GOAT

A
Leg
Bugs
Old
Einstein

A
Goat
Mocks
Einstein's leg

A
Trick
Sticks
A
Kick
At
Einstein

Einstein

Stops

And

Nods

SENTENCE MIXTURE

No time of the year
No year
No time

No heat
No warmth
No coolness
No cold
No frost

No wetness
No dampness
No dryness

No light
No darkness

No din
No noise
No sound
No tone
No silence.

Schumann's Piano Concerto

Some Notes on Performance

Piano and orchestra, piano versus orchestra, piano as orchestra – the connections are manifold. J. S. Bach, the first of the great keyboard composers, was the initiator of the concerto for one, two, three and four harpsichords. At the same time in solo works such as his Italian Concerto the keyboard writing itself shows orchestral features, the first movement alternating between stretches of tutti and solo. Among Mozart's piano sonatas there are a number of pieces including the famous one in A major к. 331 that turn the piano into an outright orchestra, whereas his marvellous piano concertos clearly distinguish between the timbre of the soloist and the impact of the ensemble. In Schubert's *Wanderer Fantasy*, an orchestra is evoked with unprecedented power, thus anticipating the road to Liszt. Chopin, in contrast, stayed within his exquisite pianistic confines. While Schumann's *Symphonic Études* presented an essay in piano orchestration, the solo instrument in his A minor Concerto remains distinctly itself, assisted rather than assaulted or contradicted by the orchestra.

There are pieces of music that seem perfect on the page and stubbornly resist perfection in the concert hall. Playing

Schumann's Piano Concerto appeared to me like trying, in Chicago, to walk from Orchestra Hall to the Four Seasons Hotel. The highest floors of the Hancock Building at the end of Michigan Avenue remain visible – however, the nearer to them you come, the more they seem to recede.

When I first played the work I had no inkling that I was embarking on a risky task. I had barely started appearing with orchestras, had not encountered stage fright and was far from considering the how and why of performing. Over the next fifty years, I had ample opportunity to try to do better.

How does a player start to get acquainted with a piece? There is, above all, the composer's text, frequently corrupted by editors. And there are, in most cases, the performances one has had the opportunity to hear, performances of varying quality and competence that may leave, in a young player, a lasting imprint. In contrast, dealing with a work of new music usually means that one has to come in from the cold. When I studied Schoenberg's Piano Concerto in the 1950s, it had barely been tackled before.

There are musicians who avoid listening to the playing of others in order to develop as much as possible their own uncontaminated conception of a piece. That, to my mind, is carrying things too far. After all, one can listen critically, and learn to steer clear of what one shouldn't do. But it would also be misguided to reject what others have done for the sake of being different and 'original'. The personal imprint of a performance should be the result not of pre-meditation but of a deep familiarity with the piece.

When had I heard Schumann's Piano Concerto per-formed? My first piano teacher in Zagreb had played it and got into some trouble in the finale. Then there was Alfred Cortot's recording from 1927, and a more recent one played by Dinu Lipatti with Karajan conducting. Although Lipatti had at some stage studied with Cortot, these recordings are polar opposites. Much as I admire Cortot's superb 1933 recording of Chopin's *Préludes* I cannot count his version of the Schumann Concerto among his triumphs. It may be far from boring and present some ravishing sounds, but it is, to my ears, remarkably exaggerated, turning the work into a rather bombastic showpiece with added doublings, echo dynamics, transpositions and several gratuitous changes of tempo while ignoring many of the composer's mark-ings. Lipatti, on the other hand, handles it with impeccable poise in the neoclassical manner of his composition teacher Nadia Boulanger, who was also his occasional duet partner.

Very few piano concertos, if any, have generated such a wide variety of readings. Lipatti himself gave, in a live record-ing shortly before his death, a remarkably different, personal and warmly committed performance with Ernest Ansermet. Arturo Benedetti Michelangeli, on the other hand, in an early one with Dimitri Mitropoulos, sounds frenzied, while his much later recording with Sergiu Celibidache is noth-ing less than lethargic, and some ten minutes longer. As for my own three recordings, it needed the stepping stones of the first two to arrive at the 2001 live recording with Simon Rattle and the Vienna Philharmonic as ideal partners. My particular thanks go to the oboist and clarinettist, whose contributions in this piece are of crucial importance.

For some players, Schumann's score merely serves as raw material to be moulded *ad libitum*. What does Schumann write in his *Musikalische Haus- und Lebensregeln* (*Musical Rules for House and Life*)? 'Always play flexibly and boldly! Remember that two bars rendered in the same tempo are proof of a lack of imagination.' No, I made that up. Here is what he really said: 'Play in time. The playing of some virtuosos resembles a drunkard walking. Don't follow their example.' I do not see why after the opening *allegro* bars the *cantabile* theme should be played in a markedly different and slower tempo. In this work, essential tempo changes are indicated clearly enough except, obviously, in the cadenza.

After hearing various performances, what was it that in Schumann's Concerto I heard in myself? Something noble and ardently lyrical but not recklessly rhapsodic. There should be, or so I felt, the possibility of avoiding both hyper-Romantic hubris and a streamlined fluency that makes the music resemble Hummel's or Mendelssohn's. Schumann, to my knowledge, was neither Russian, nor Polish, nor French. He was steeped in the 'German' tradition, and deeply admired Bach, Beethoven and Schubert. His Piano Concerto may be taken as a ravishing link between Beethoven and Brahms. The first movement's tempo indication *Allegro affettuoso* is frequently misunderstood: *affettuoso* means neither passionate nor affected, but affectionate. Only once, during the development section, is *passionato* asked for, and linked to an increase of tempo. I do not blindly adhere to metronome markings but I think that the speeds Schumann suggests in this work give a fair indication of the character of each movement. The fluency of the middle movement's *Andantino grazioso* reminds us that we should not mistake it for a slow movement in the traditional sense, as some German pianists did, and that the *espressivo* cantilena of the cellos can be conveyed with discreet rapture. One of Clara Schumann's English students, Fanny Davies, recorded the work in the 1930s. Her *Andantino* is the most fluent of all. But with all due respect for a performance that ought to have to come from the horse's mouth, I cannot accept her lack of flexibility: *ritardandi* at transitions are frequently ignored. The exceptionally fine finale, on the other hand, is less a dashing virtuoso piece than a dancing *vivace* that should be kept firmly under control. Its enthusiasm must never go overboard. Clara Schumann rejoiced that Robert had finally produced for her a 'bravura piece'. But the pianistic effort that goes into practising such a piece easily results in a *prestissimo* romp pleasing those members of the audience who, metaphorically speaking, listen to music with a stopwatch. In technically gifted players, there is a momentum that unleashes speed like an avalanche. Ensemble players, of course, have to resist this. Why shouldn't the soloist?

It was a noble gesture of Liszt to invite Clara, when she resumed her solo career after Robert's death, to perform the A minor Concerto in Weimar on 27 October 1854 under his own baton. That Clara lacked any understanding for Liszt's music didn't prevent him from generously appreciating her playing, and warmly admiring the compositions of her husband. Liszt reproached himself in later years for not having more actively supported Schumann's music as a virtuoso.

How seriously should we take a composer's markings? The question immediately arises: which composer's? There are those who precisely imagine how their music should sound, the most extreme example I know being György Kurtág. At the other end of the spectrum, there are composers who leave a great deal to the soloist. (Works for ensembles are in general marked more carefully.) A paragon of completeness, clarity, practicality and precision is Béla Bartók. An example of vagueness would be Busoni, who himself treated the works by others quite freely, maintaining that writing down a composition already amounts to a transcription. And there is Mozart, who in his piano works offers both varieties of markings: none, and too many. Reger, Schoenberg and Berg tended to overmark. The composer who with impressive skill and confidence asks for the essential is Beethoven.

To ignore his markings – providing the player understands them properly – is the performer's loss. According to my ripe-old-age experience, some 90 per cent of them make eminent sense. Chopin's markings can be quite confusing: look at all the variants within the contemporary editions of his own works. It is not entirely surprising that he has been treated in cavalier fashion by many Chopin specialists. But it would be a mistake to discount his markings right away. Many of them make good sense. The same applies to Schumann. To be sure, there are odd blunders, including the prescription *Durchweg leise zu halten* (Softly throughout) in the third movement of his C major *Fantasie* Op. 17, a movement that includes two glorious climaxes. Schumann composed at great speed, yet many of his markings are more plausible than we would like to allow.

After the Baroque era, the great composers have been gracious enough to leave us hints as to how their music should be performed. These instructions are never complete. But they seemed to them important enough to be put on paper. They are propositions, sometimes maybe to the composers themselves, but they do come from the source. In principle, the composer knows better. The fact that Rachmaninov or Prokofiev or even Bartók may have done some things differently when they performed does not speak against their notation. I think Bartók's printed tempi in his Suite Op. 14 make better sense than the considerably faster ones on his recording. On the other hand, I have always felt that some of Beethoven's own metronome figures for the 'Hammer-klavier' Sonata Op. 106 are detrimental to this great work and the clarity of its perception.

There are some rare instances where the performer has to defend a piece against the composer's own playing. Tempi shouldn't be decided by blindly following a metronome figure from the outset. Familiarity with all the components of a composition is needed before the player can settle on tempi that have the capability of housing them all.

In great music, markings of dynamics and articulation are not just a cosmetic arrangement on the surface to be disregarded at will. Most likely, they are connected to the character and atmosphere, the life and blood of a work. Are you one of those performers whose aim it is to float in a condition of ecstasy without rhyme or reason? Schumann's Concerto deserves better.

Christian Morgenstern

THE KNEE

translated by Alfred Brendel

A knee walks lonely through the world.
It's nothing but a knee!
It's not a tent! It's not a tree!
It's nothing but a knee.

There was a man who in the war
was maimed from head to feet.
The knee alone remained unscathed –
A miracle indeed.

Since then it's walking through the world.
It's nothing but a knee.
It's not a tent. It's not a tree.
It's nothing but a knee.

DAS GROSSE LALULA

Kroklokwafzi? Semememi!
Seiokrontro – prafriplo:
Bifzi, bafzi; hulalemi:
quasti basti bo . . .
Lalu lalu lalu lalu la!

Hontraruru miromente
zasku zes rü rü?
Entepente, leiolente
klekwapufzi lü?
Lalu lalu lalu lala la!

Simarat kos malzlpempu
silzuzankunkrei (;)!
Marjomar dos: Quempu Lempu
Siri Suri Sei []!
Lalu lalu lalu lalu la!

THE DOES' PRAYER

translated by Max Knight

The does, as the hour grows late,
med-it-ate;
med-it-nine;
med-i-ten;
med-eleven;
med-twelve;
mednight!

The does, as the hour grows late,
meditate.
They fold their little toesies,
the doesies.

My Musical Life

In England, where I have lived for decades, people of some repute are expected to produce an autobiography. I shall never do so – I'm too fond of the truth for that – and there are many things that fascinate me more than my own personality. In this short memoir, I shall concentrate on my *musical* life. I do not believe that artistic merits can be derived from, or explained by, an artist's private existence.

Nevertheless, let me start with my parents. Neither of the two families included artists or intellectuals. And, in spite of exhaustive searching, I have so far not managed to track down any Jewish ancestors. My grandfather's connection with music consisted in the fact that Gustav and Alma Mahler learned how to ride a bicycle at his cycling school. These were the times when bicycles were equipped with one big and one small wheel. Both my mother and my father belonged to German-speaking minorities in countries that, as they felt, treated them poorly. Both had taken a few piano lessons, part of a bourgeois routine that I also experienced. As a little child I had been taught a number of folk songs by my nanny before I could operate the record player at a hotel on the Adriatic island of Krk. Among the records there was an operetta aria bellowed out by the tenor Jan Kiepura. It proclaimed that 'whether blond or brunette

I love all women'. A nice one to sing along to. In those days, the gramophone had still to be wound up, and, when it was, out rang a 1920s Berlin hit posing the question, 'What is Meyers doing on the Himalayas?'

My parents were loving and reliable. That counts for a lot. For the rest, there wasn't too much we had in common – as I discovered as a teenager – which had its advantages since I got used to finding out things for myself, a state of affairs that would become permanent.

My two piano teachers, ladies both, one in Croatian Zagreb, the other in the Styrian town of Graz, left me sufficient musical leeway. The first invested a lot of energy in strengthening my little fingers, for which I am grateful; the other one told me that I was tense and needed to relax. She didn't tell me how but it was interesting to find out by myself. Towards the end of the war there was an extended gap in my piano playing because there was no piano. With my mother, I fled from the Russian army that was occupying Styria, and returned there only when it withdrew. Between fifteen and seventeen I made up for much of what I had missed out on off my own bat. I lived in a medieval house in Graz where I shared a room with a cousin who studied medicine and seemed to have been oblivious to noise. I composed, drew and painted, wrote sonnets and practised the piano. And I read a great deal. A public library facing the house had retained, in its cellars, an ample supply of pre-war literature. When I turned sixteen my piano teacher told me I should now continue on my own, and give a first public recital. I should also audition for the great Swiss pianist Edwin Fischer, which I did the following year. Three of his masterclasses that I attended during the Lucerne Festivals made an impact that lasts to this day. I also met Eduard Steuermann, the pupil of Busoni and Schoenberg. Apart from these encounters I studied on my own.

The programme for my first solo recital in Graz, as well as its title, was devised by myself. It was called 'The Fugue in Piano Literature', and would have frightened me in later years. At that stage, I didn't know what 'nerves' were. The success of this debut calmed, for the time being, the nerves of my anxious mother.

In 1949 I appeared with an orchestra for the first time. It was nothing less than Beethoven's so-called, and mis-named, 'Emperor' Concerto that I performed in Graz in the Stefaniensaal, a concert hall I still consider one of the finest. Among other piano concertos that I tackled from early on were Weber's *Konzertstück*, the Schumann Concerto, Liszt's Second Concerto and Mozart's K. 503. It was a happy time without televisions, mobile phones, computers, Facebook and Twitter. The voices of Hitler and Goebbels no longer invaded the loudspeakers, and many people, after the end of the horrible war, were sceptical and obliging. It was also an exciting time as all the contemporary art that had been inaccessible gradually resurfaced. My curiosity for everything that is new in art has stayed with me throughout my life.

From 1950 I lived in Vienna, at first with a great-aunt who only after several years allowed me to hire a piano. Consequently, I had to throw myself on the mercy of friends and acquaintances in order to be able to practise for an hour or two. This had the benefit that I didn't practise too much. A pianist can ruin himself by too much practice. The house in which my great-aunt lived was, at the time, one of the many Viennese buildings that provided running water only outside the apartment, to be collected with buckets.

In the early 1950s, three things happened. First, I started to make records, an activity that would continue for half a century. Second, I did a concert tour of Spain and Portugal with a chamber orchestra that, apart from the conductor, consisted entirely of women. From Vienna, we drove in a bus covering ten thousand kilometres in four weeks. There was snow on the Montserrat while, in the valley below, the almond trees bloomed. Then came an invitation to accompany a Greek violinist in Athens. The trip by rail from Vienna through Yugoslavia lasted fifty-two hours. After the recital, the violinist said, 'Can't you stay on for another ten days? I'm supposed to play with the Athens orchestra as a soloist, and I would like you to take over my engagement.' Thus, I did my first performance of Mozart's Concerto in D minor. I borrowed the score, which still contained his written notes, from a pupil of Artur Schnabel.

Vienna, in the early post-war years, was popular with a number of small and medium-sized American record companies. Among the first works that I recorded for a tiny label were late Liszt pieces and Busoni's *Fantasia contrappuntistica*, music that nobody knew. The record catalogue in those days was fairly thin. Fees were small, and recording contracts ridiculous. But I was grateful to have something that kept my head above water. At the age of twenty-five I made my first record for VOX, a company that later called itself Turnabout and kept me busy over the next ten years. My first VOX recording included, besides Balakirev's *Islamey*, Stravinsky's *Petrushka Suite* and Mussorgsky's *Pictures at an Exhibition*.

As well as recording a few Mozart concertos and some of Liszt's paraphrases, I embarked on a recording of Beethoven's complete piano works. It was a fortunate decision to start with his smaller sets of variations. They added something important to my knowledge of Beethoven: I realised that the purported Titan was also able to compose with a light hand, enjoy being witty, and demonstrate his own individual version of gracefulness. The player can learn to characterise, to give each variation its own specific flavour – just as long as it is not one of those variation works that retain the character of the theme.

It was by chance that I finished the first of my three recordings of Beethoven's 32 sonatas on my thirty-second birthday. There followed many concert performances of the sonata cycle, an undertaking that needed four or five attempts to settle down. Up until the age of seventy I particularly enjoyed doing cycles of the five Beethoven concertos. For the VOX recording of the Fifth Concerto, Zubin Mehta was my very young conductor, facing the Vienna Symphony for the first time. Later I would often join Zubin in Europe, North America and Israel.

In the late 1950s, Michael Gielen made me learn the Piano Concerto by Arnold Schoenberg, which we then performed in Warsaw at the first international festival of contemporary music that had ever been mounted in Eastern Europe. The public, who had never heard this kind of music before, made us repeat the last movement. Nadia Boulanger, the famous Parisian composition teacher who had trained some of the Polish composers, sat sulking in the balcony. She was completely devoted to Stravinsky, who at the time had not yet discovered the music of the Second Vienna School. Warsaw was in those days a city in ruins above which towered the gigantic Palace of Culture. It had been erected by the Russians and is still there – too huge to be demolished. I've played the Schoenberg Concerto 68 times, made three recordings of it, and given premiere performances on three continents. It has remained a problem piece but one whose problems repay close consideration.

Meanwhile, Mozart's piano concertos and Schubert's sonatas had become, as part of my repertoire, more and more important. In the years after the war sonatas by Schubert were rarely programmed. A performance of his four-movement A minor Sonata by Wilhelm Kempff helped to open my ears. Played in Vienna's biggest concert hall, it showed me that these works need a bigger space to fully come to life, and that they should be played orchestrally, dramatically and cohesively. In this, the late sonatas differ from his impromptus, *moments musicaux* or piano chamber music, which, as it were, emerge *from* the piano, whereas the sonatas impose an orchestra on it. With the *Wanderer Fantasy* Schubert strikingly demonstrated that the work had gone far beyond the capabilities of contemporary keyboard instruments. The modern piano is so much better equipped to be turned into an orchestra with its sound, colour and dynamic range. In the 1960s, German television gave me the opportunity to make thirteen films encompassing the last seven years of Schubert's life, from the *Wanderer Fantasy* to his final sonatas. Subsequently, I often performed these works over four evenings. Incidentally, the timespan within which Schubert composed his greatest instrumental works seems to coincide precisely with his affliction with syphilis. It took some time before the received opinion that Schubert's music was too lyrical, too long and lacking in shape was left behind. Today, his sonatas are firmly established in the repertoire.

Since 1971, I have lived in London. That means that this is the place where I keep most of my books and music. But I still do a lot of travelling. The fact that I was born in northern Moravia, went to Yugoslavia as a child and moved from Zagreb to Austria before settling in London, combined with the life of a touring pianist – such a peripatetic existence has always seemed to me a blessing. It didn't, however, need the Brexit vote to remind me that I'm a European.

I value a certain degree of independence. I have never been part of an institution. I never organised a series of events or founded a club. The only crowd – to speak with Elias Canetti – that I am not wary of is the public of concerts and theatre.

There were a number of reasons to settle in London. Before the disappearance of the Iron Curtain, Vienna felt to me rather provincial. Two things convinced me of London's status as a musical metropolis: the Promenade Concerts and the Third Programme of the BBC. Where else does one find a series like the 'Proms' where throughout the whole summer up to eight thousand people gather to listen, evening after evening, to orchestral concerts that are also broadcast live? Both the Proms and the Third Programme were masterminded by Sir William Glock, a pupil of Schnabel. Glock had succeeded in freeing both institutions from their insularity, and in internationalising the performances of contemporary music. Before that, the Proms, gossip had it, were the only place where British composers could hear their work twice. The famous echo of the Albert Hall was later eliminated by round blue panels suspended from the ceiling. It is only fair to say that, since then, British music has become a great deal more international as well. It's hard to imagine a more attentive audience than the standing 'Promenaders'. Confronted with the contrasting elements of the hall's interior, a French architect friend observed, 'Half Colosseum, half brothel.' (You may remember the red velvet draperies.) The Albert Hall turned out to be one of my musical homes. I played there 35 times including, within orchestral concerts, solo works such as Beethoven's *Diabelli Variations* and Schubert's *Wanderer Fantasy*. But I never attended the final night. It displays a chauvinism that is not to my taste.

The records I had made up till then were for smaller labels. A Beethoven recital at the Queen Elizabeth Hall – not one of my best – triggered a second phase of my career and mobilised three of the big companies, of which, for the rest of my concert life, Philips became my home address.

It seemed clear to me what I would do after my final concerts in Vienna in December 2008: lecturing, presenting readings of my poetry, coaching string quartets, writing, travelling. What remained open was how long the impact of my playing would continue to resonate. I count myself lucky that my recordings, even most of the earlier ones, still seem to be available. There have been musicians who in no time fell into oblivion.

What further remained to be seen was how my health would hold up. Here, there were surprises of which the

breakdown of my hearing six years ago was the most incon-
venient.

From the 1970s, I frequently went to America doing solo
recitals mostly in the spring and appearing with orchestras
mostly in their summer residencies. One of them I became
particularly familiar with was Ravinia. There, the Chicago
Orchestra plays right next door to a railway station, which
made Sir Thomas Beecham remark that this was the only
railway station with a resident symphony orchestra. An
exceedingly noisy old-fashioned train invariably pulled
into the station during the slow movement of my piano
concerto. It is rather bizarre but not without its own peculiar charm that in these summer concerts music should
be performed in the open air for thousands of people,
some of whom were sitting on the lawn. The fluctuations
of temperature were remarkable. I have seen the audience
wrapped in blankets. On the other hand I have played
three Beethoven concertos in one evening at 100°F and 90
per cent humidity.

Just once I dared to play a concerto without rehearsal.
At five o'clock in the afternoon the telephone rang, and the
manager of the Royal Philharmonic Orchestra gave me the
news that his soloist for the evening had just cancelled.
Couldn't I come over and play something? It turned out
that a couple of months earlier the orchestra had been on

tour with Mozart's D minor Concerto. So I called a cab and, after a short conversation with the conductor, played the piece with Riccardo Chailly.

In my experience, most conductors are helpful as long as they realise that the soloist thoroughly knows the score and isn't asking for something absurd. Among the friendly conductors there were those who retained everything I had told them, and others who let me know, after I'd said three things, 'Don't tell me a fourth – I won't remember it anyway.' Very old conductors usually need to be accompanied by the soloist. There were only a few conductors I avoided playing with, not for personal reasons but because I knew that we were musically incompatible. I much enjoyed working with those with whom one could set up performances properly over a number of years. I am thinking above all of my various Beethoven cycles with James Levine and Simon Rattle.

It is nice if conductors try to accommodate the soloist. But there are also a few who cultivate the habit of cutting short the soloist's rehearsal time. This is bad behaviour, and provokes in the soloist a kind of murderous urge. Young players in particular are sometimes on the receiving end of such treatment.

I have often said that I have learned a great deal from listening to singers and conductors. The reason is that, for me, the sound of the piano is not the goal but the point of departure. It has to be transformed. To make the piano sing, to turn it into an orchestra is both possible and necessary.

There are pianists who are not comfortable with an orchestra. They would rather steer clear from the constraints of ensemble playing and develop their own unfettered notion of rhythm and tempo. Is piano literature in its incomparable profusion not destined to liberate the player from superfluous shackles? Are not all those fantasias, toccatas, cadenzas and recitative-like passages its quintessence?

Chopin, I willingly concede, is such a soloist's composer. With some restrictions, young Schumann and young Liszt may also qualify. As for the rest, great piano composers have all been ensemble composers, some of them first and foremost. Their piano works are often closely connected to their orchestral, vocal and chamber music and to the discipline of rhythmic cooperation with all its necessary and possible flexibility as embodied by a good conductor.

It seems to me highly unlikely that a great composer would sport two basically different rhythmic conceptions, one for solo and one for ensemble playing. My yardstick for rhythm and tempo is taken from the great orchestras and the best conductors. Tempo modifications that are not conductable, and unavailable to orchestral musicians, will, on the piano, be mostly superfluous. There are soloists who think that they may, or even need to, demonstrate all the liberties imaginable when there are no other players around who would get in the way of their spontaneity. I personally would much rather go the other way and listen, before playing a Beethoven sonata, to a good performance of a Beethoven quartet, not least with regards to respecting the score. Four musicians who have to play together are facing the same markings that, if they use a good edition, have been written down by the composer himself.

In my younger years, great pianists were sometimes divided into two groups: Chopin players who were dealing predominantly with the Polish composer, and the performers of a larger, mostly Central European repertoire. It seemed rather obvious that, in order to play Chopin well, you had to specialise. It also helped when such pianists had Eastern European names such as Paderewski, Koczalski, Brailowsky, Uninsky, Niedzielski, Czerny-Stefańska, or Pachmann and Friedman. What counted was a highly personal refinement that took hold of the player to such a degree that it was hardly applicable to other composers. I had studied a fair number of Chopin's works but soon noticed that the Central European orientation was the one I would pursue. In the 1960s, I made an exception and focused my attention on Chopin's relatively neglected polonaises, which I coupled with a selection of Liszt's Hungarian rhapsodies. I had been playing Liszt since my earliest performances at the Conservatory in Graz. Liszt's music, at that time, did not have a good reputation. To me, the best of it has remained compelling enough throughout a lifetime. Dealing with Liszt, the pianist will be able to realise that technical skill should never be in the foreground. Liszt should not be treated as a piano circus but as music. Virtuosity never ought to be an end in itself but a means of expression. There are, among the Hungarian rhapsodies, pieces of genius provided that they are played with the necessary conviction.

The last great Chopin player in the old sense was Alfred Cortot. His recording of the *24 Préludes* from 1933 has to me remained a miracle. Throughout my life, it has never lost anything of its phenomenal freshness and daring. Meanwhile, Chopin, the bird of paradise, has been swallowed up by the musical mainstream.

When I repeat that I have profited most from listening to singers and conductors, I do not want to diminish the lasting impact of a number of pianists. In my most excitable early years of listening it was particularly Edwin Fischer, Alfred Cortot and Wilhelm Kempff who in concerts and on recordings gave me an inkling of what I myself hoped later to accomplish. The playing of these three pianists was remarkably uneven. Kempff, a master of atmospheric playing, could be called an Aeolian harp – he sounded wonderful when the right wind blew. But the very best of these pianists' performances have continued to serve as a yardstick. What, in all their diversity, did they have in common? They were great masters of sound and *cantabile*, and they were magicians of immediacy. When Fischer played another veil was lifted from the soul. You witnessed a combination of seraphic simplicity, refinement and nervous turmoil. In the best of Cortot's recordings of Chopin's *Préludes*, each of the 24 pieces has a unique, clearly distinguishable profile. At the same time, they are played as a cycle, in one big breath that ties the disparate characters together. The very first bars would at once establish the basic character of each piece with complete assurance; it was as if a kaleidoscope would be shaken, and the new constellation was instantly there. All three pianists were also great chamber musicians, two of them professional conductors as well: Cortot was responsible for important orchestral premieres in Paris; Fischer toured with his chamber orchestra. What they also shared was the need to create wider contexts, to connect, to show how one thing leads to another, and the first note to the last. Wilhelm Furtwängler, Bruno Walter, Otto Klemperer, some of the great conductors among their contemporaries, struck me in a similar way. It may have been a symptom of this generation that it didn't dissect but rather bound the components together. Listen to one of the most moving examples of this style, Edwin Fischer's performance of the *Largo* of Bach's F minor Concerto.

There are different ways of establishing a career. The early, sensational one as the winner of a major competition with extensive concert appearances and a recording contract does not guarantee continuous success. The danger is that an avalanche of publicity is all too speedily released and a flood of engagements descends on the young player who needs time to assemble a repertoire, learn about concert life from the inside and find a way of negotiating from the age of twenty to thirty as a human being. A gradual build-up is necessary, the development should continue, the interest of orchestras, the esteem of conductors and, last but not least, the response of the public should lead to re-engagements. The word development is crucial – the debut of a pianist, even if brilliant, may just give a hint of his or her talent while some violinists already at a young age are able to display a mastery that is available to pianists only later. And the public sometimes even has to get used to the way a performer looks. A pianist who onstage cuts a good figure and doesn't move a facial muscle will have an easier time than those who are prone to producing grimaces, including myself. My own career, despite my having won a prize in 1949, was not sudden or sensational but progressed step by step. In hindsight, I'm very grateful for this. My potential was able to unfold in a style that was consistent with my largely independent way of working and thinking. Unlike many others I have never been impatient. I knew there was a talent but time would tell how sound it was and where it would lead. Of course, talent is not everything. What is needed as well is a good constitution, self-confidence and self-criticism, ambition and persistence, preferably without fanaticism, a good memory, good nerves, the gift of concentration, the readiness and joy of transmitting something to others, and sufficient scepticism not to take oneself all too seriously. One needs *gravitas* and lightness, flexibility – an openness to the many characters of the music – and, of course, luck.

One of my strokes of luck was that the concert agents who took care of me were ones whose patience matched my own. There was, on the whole, enough stability in the organisation of my concert life to suggest that in this profession, more than in many others, it seemed possible to be, and to remain, a relatively free person.

I had already heard Julius Patzak, a quite distinctive tenor of around sixty, sing *Winterreise* in Vienna with a lovely Austrian diction. When I was in my mid-twenties, I got a telephone call asking me to accompany him in a *Lieder* recital. It was my first collaboration with a singer. The programme included Janáček, Bartók and a song by Richard Strauss with millions of notes in the piano part. Perhaps this was too outlandish for Viennese accompanists. There were two rehearsals. In the first one, Patzak was sight-reading while in the second he mainly smoked. Then came years where I joined the baritone Hermann Prey at music festivals. Once we even did an actual four-week tour in his Citroën. After the first concert in Amsterdam we were invited to the house of a musicologist. We sat down at a table on which a small plate with biscuits was displayed and started to laugh when our host said, 'I trust you've had dinner already.' On that day, quite a few things had already happened. In our hotel the elevator was under construction, and the page turner had forgotten to turn the pages.

Dietrich Fischer-Dieskau, my next singer, had acquired the habit of not just appearing with accompanists but if possible with piano soloists. Under his auspices, the accompanist mutated into a partner. It was evident that he valued suggestions and new ideas coming from the pianist. He sang with open ears, and his mastery was so sovereign that he always appeared completely in command. Fischer-Dieskau's breathing technique was so superior that one hardly ever noticed him breathing in. The clarity of his diction was tailor-made for big halls: he was the only *Lieder* singer who on an international scale could fill large halls. One of our *Winterreise* performances, at the Royal Opera House, Covent Garden, remains to me particularly unforgettable. After another one in Lockenhaus he instantly disappeared, and was carried away by a helicopter. The reason? He was being pursued by a woman with a gun.

The third singer, also a baritone, was Matthias Goerne, once again, a supremely alert artist. The unity and intensity of his music-making was never in question. Meanwhile it has become common practice to open the piano lid completely, something that in chamber music and *Lieder* has never been to my taste – or to that of other musicians a few decades ago. It is probably due to the request of sound engineers who claim that they can get a better recorded piano sound. Alas, the listener in the concert hall will easily get the impression of the singer being inside the piano, and not in front. I have always used the quarter stick, even in live recordings.

For me singing, *cantabile*, is at the heart of music, one of its constitutive secrets. It is joined by telling articulation and, on the operatic stage, by gesture and movement. In Mozart's piano concertos, the player may, at times, turn into an imaginary operatic figure. Recently, a lot has been written about musical speech. The rhetorical element should, however, not dominate but rather complement the *cantabile*. Plasticity and clarity of diction will be an asset to pianists as well.

Apart from the singers I worked with I also drew inspiration from listening to opera, and records. In the 1950s, before the Vienna State Opera house had been restored, a famous Mozart ensemble performed at the Theater an der Wien. Elisabeth Schwarzkopf, Sena Jurinac and Irmgard Seefried were the leading ladies whose memorable appearances on stage have merged in my memory with the timbre of their voices. Soon, they were joined by Christa Ludwig. The duo of Schwarzkopf and Ludwig remained to me the perfect pairing of Fiordiligi and Dorabella, with Graziella Sciutti as the ideal Despina. Among tenors, Julius Patzak and Anton Dermota regularly appeared, and Erich Kunz was a peerless Papageno. Josef Krips or Karl Böhm conducted. Fritz Busch, whom Vienna finally got round to inviting, died all too soon. It took quite some time before the musicians and the public became used to the proper execution of appoggiaturas. Just in case you're interested: appoggiaturas are those two-note groups in which the first of two repeated notes has to be sung or played – in the Baroque style – at a different pitch (usually higher). Opera direction at that time did not offer commentaries, paraphrases or parodies of works but stagings that communicated even to the uninitiated what was actually going on.

During Karajan's time in Vienna I witnessed memorable performances of Italian Opera. *Aida*, *Otello*, *Falstaff*, but also *Carmen*, were, as I found, Karajan's particular domain. Under his baton, Leontyne Price sang Aida and Regina Resnik Carmen – one of the few realisations of this role that I ever found convincing. At the Theater an der Wien Furtwängler had conducted *Tristan*. How the opening moment of each act immediately conveyed the basic character of the music was unforgettable – one can verify this with the help of his great recording with the Philharmonia Orchestra. Of inestimable value to me were the recordings of two dramatic sopranos: Lotte Lehmann and Maria Callas. Lotte Lehmann came to Vienna as an old lady to give a singing class to which the Viennese singing teachers did not send a single student. The way she sang, or rather suggested, *Frauenliebe und -leben*, because there was hardly any voice left, brought all of us to tears.

*

As a twenty-year-old I hoped to achieve something by the time I reached fifty. When I turned fifty I noticed that there were still a few things to do. In my sixties, there was a minor interruption. While performing both Brahms concertos on a concert tour I overstrained my left arm. A reassessment of my repertoire that had so far contained a remarkable number of highly athletic pieces had become necessary. It remained to be seen how the public would react. But they were gracious about it and seemed to go along with my opinion that Haydn, Mozart, Beethoven and Schubert had contributed a reasonable number of substantial piano works anyway.

In addition, my repertoire had included a fair selection of works by Liszt and Schumann while Bach, Russian and French music were mostly excluded. A Bach recording for Philips was an exception. During 1976 I had played a pro-gramme that at first glance might seem all too daring: it combined works by Bach and Liszt (Hungarian rhapsodies) with Beethoven's *Diabelli Variations*. While recording a few Liszt pieces, I finished one day early and took advantage of the spare time by recording, among other works, Bach's *Chromatic Fantasia and Fugue* and his unpredictable A minor *Fantasia* as well as the *Italian Concerto*. I'm glad that this Bach recording came about, if only by accident.

Why then didn't I play Bach both more often and more regularly? There had been an upsurge of period perfor-mances that had rejected modern instruments. Another, quite different reason was the impact of Edwin Fischer's Bach playing, for which finding an equivalent seemed to me a very tall order. Fortunately for us pianists the rights of the modern grand have meanwhile been re-established.

Concert tours took me repeatedly to Latin America, Australia, Israel and Japan. I had stopped going to Latin America by 1961. The organisation of these trips was to a scarcely imaginable extent left to chance, and pianos were bad. Besides, I was busy enough elsewhere. I particularly remember a recital in San Salvador where a rat appeared on stage, and the conclusion of my final tour. Before my departure from this continent I was supposed to play three concerts in Buenos Aires: Schoenberg's Piano Concerto at the Teatro Colón, a benefit recital for the Austrian Embassy, and two Mozart concertos at the Mozarteo. We rehearsed Schoenberg and the notes were gradually becoming recognisable when Pope John XXIII died and all 'entertainment' was cancelled. First, there came a telephone call from the Austrian Ambassador, who told me that the recital should nevertheless go ahead – this would definitely have met with the approval of the deceased. But he urged me to modify the programme and eliminate the Schubert sonata in order to avoid frivolous associations with *Lilac Time*. I assured him that the big A minor Sonata was a tragic work and played it, of course. The next call came from my Argentinian agent telling me that he knew that I was unable to prolong my stay and therefore had the following proposal. After the end of the period of mourning I should first get the Mozart concertos out of the way and then be driven over to the Teatro Colón for the Schoenberg. Thus it happened that I appeared on the same evening in two different houses with two different orchestras and conductors.

The tour of Australia that followed was splendidly organised. The man in charge was a certain Mr Moses whose hobby was chopping wood. In his office, there was a cupboard full of axes. In order to demonstrate how sharp-edged they were, he selected one of them, rolled up his shirt-sleeve and shaved off a few hairs from his arm. In Ballarat, a particularly chilly Australian place, I told the freezing public that I just wished I had an axe on hand to demolish their concert grand.

In Israel I had to do what I never did anywhere else – to play six days a week. Fortunately, there was the Sabbath, which provided me and the orchestra with a free day. I was deeply touched that at the hundredth anniversary celebrations for Arthur Rubinstein I was invited to participate as the only non-Jewish pianist.

When playing in Japan I never failed to visit Kyoto to discover some new temples, and to go to Nara, the wonderful old capital, where many deer roam the streets trying to steal chocolate from ladies' handbags while stags rummage in the dustbins.

*

Next to a great many appearances with orchestras and at least as many in recitals there were the recordings, the number of which, in hindsight, has surprised me. It is a strange feeling looking back at so many records: offspring, some of which never really grow up. My studio recordings for Philips were more and more supplemented by live recordings without me having a marked preference for either. I became accustomed to playing in the studio with an intensity similar to that in a concert hall while live recordings turned out to be mostly happy finds among the radio recordings of my concerts. In the studio one is able to listen to playback, react critically, repeat and edit, while what counts in a live performance is the risk involved of getting through it all in one go. Both have their advantages. No one, I think, would be able to spot the edits in my studio recordings, if any. The precondition is that the performance needs to have a concept. My warmest thanks go to my producers for their committed assistance.

Alongside my musical responsibilities my other career, that of a writer, gradually developed to become a second creative life. I wrote about music and matters connected to my piano playing until my poems surprised me. Obviously, they were part of my personality. But they showed an alter ego. I would like to claim that there are a number of dimensions in myself that supplement each other – serious and non-serious, sense and nonsense, doubt and conviction. Only in contradiction does the world seem to become a little less absurd. There are, in me, a number of houses and doors. Whoever looks for the Dadaist in my piano playing has tried the wrong door.

As a writing pianist I was called a 'savage philosopher at the piano' or even, in America, branded as an intellectual. That's what happens if you publish books, wear spectacles, and don't play Rachmaninov. But in all this, the feeling for and seeking out of musical elements have always been more important to me. Anyone who has watched me teaching knows that I do not waste too much time on dogma or analytical explanation but work precisely on the notes, on their value, colour and nuance, on balance and cohesion. Over many years I particularly enjoyed it when string quartets sought my advice. The fact that I'm not a string player myself didn't seem an obstacle but even an advantage. My awareness of what string players can do has developed from my own piano playing.

Strenuous as the life of a travelling pianist can be, there is no shortage of surprises. During my orchestral debut in North America the middle D kept sticking in Brahms's D minor Concerto – I had to constantly lift up the key during my playing. But that was not all. In the course of two further trips to Montreal, there was a similar mechanical jinx at work. While practising at Meadowbrook, the summer pavilion of the Detroit Orchestra, a bird flew into the pavilion's roof and thudded down onto the floor, dead, right next to me. During a Beethoven recital at Carnegie Hall I heard a strange noise between two movements. It originated from a dog that was being ushered out with its escort, who apparently kept protesting, 'This is Mr Brendel's dog!' In Cali, a Colombian city of ill repute, the entire pedal came down at the final chord of Schumann's *Symphonic Études*. And in Algiers, where French soldiers with machine-guns patrolled the street corners and the musicians of the orchestra were searched for weapons, I was asked to play Liszt's *Totentanz*, followed by Beethoven's *Choral Fantasia* that had been provided with a French text in which the word 'Patrie' appeared as often as possible.

After my final concert with the Vienna Philharmonic in December 2008, lectures on music and performance have taken up some of my time. I have given talks on Mozart, Beethoven, Schubert and the sometimes misunderstood and misrepresented Liszt. Other subjects that have been of interest to me for many years were character and humour in music as well as certain habits and dogmas of present-day performance practice. When, in Stuttgart, I described Beethoven's *Diabelli Variations* as a compendium of musical humour, I was fiercely attacked by a newspaper. It seems that the idea of a Beethoven who in his late works had left behind all that is worldly and is floating transfigured somewhere above the clouds has remained precious to some minds along with the conviction that the comical is something inferior and ill suited to those of a serious cast of mind. Of course, there are also overreactions on the other side. Young musicians who try to express musical humour easily exaggerate.

I concluded my pianistic career without tears. This should not be interpreted as a lack of musical commitment. I loved to play but I was ready for the farewell. Sixty years of this activity seemed sufficient, and it was to me of paramount importance to stop as long as I was still capable of monitoring my sense of rhythm and nuance.

In some respect these last years have been more demanding than the concert years before. Whereas then I was able to focus on a limited amount of works per season, now nearly each appearance brings new challenges. Lectures, conversations, readings of my poetry, where I vary the selection and sequence, the writing of new essays, the coaching of chamber music or the preparations for an undertaking such as the Berlin Homage have kept me up to the mark. To which I should add the reading of books, magazines such as the *New York Review*, and newspapers with their sinister reports on the global situation. But I still manage to laugh – not as much as before but enough to survive. As long as you can find things funny, not everything is lost. I feel awe and enormous gratitude when I recall how Beethoven and Schubert, Haydn and Mozart, Bach and Handel have imbued me with energy and rapture, how all that is new in music has nourished my curiosity, and how the arts, literature, theatre and film brought about epiphanies but also critical discrimination. There would be some good reason to talk about love. But I promised not to become too personal. Listen to Schubert's Impromptu in G flat.

Brief Nonsense Bibliography

Among the publications on nonsense and the grotesque, I particularly took note of Winfried Menninghaus, *Lob des Unsinns* (Suhrkamp); Susan Stuart, *Nonsense* (The Johns Hopkins University Press); Noel Malcolm, *The Origins of English Nonsense* (Harper Collins); Alfred Liede, *Dichtung als Spiel*, 2 vols (de Gruyter); Karl Friedrich Flögel, *Geschichte des Grotesk-Komischen* (Die Bibliophilen Taschenbücher), and Philip Thompson's splendid investigation *The Grotesque* (Methuen), not to forget the special issue of *Merkur: Lachen. Über westliche Zivilisation* (Klett Cotta).

The Authors of Nonsense Texts

Charles (Karl) Amberg (1894–1964) wrote texts for cabaret songs and operettas in the Berlin of the 1920s in conjunction with the composer Fred Raymond.

Hans (Jean) Arp (1886–1966), Alsatian–French–German poet, painter, graphic artist and influential sculptor, co-founder of Zurich's Dadaism, later member of the group Abstraction-Creation, and Surrealist. Dada poetry is, in Arp's words, 'a text world that has nothing to do with our world'. The poems of *Wolkenpumpe* he called collages. Their main purpose was to be accidental.

Ernst Jandl (1925–2000), Austrian poet and dramatist who acquired late fame with writings that include realism and experiment, concrete poetry and texts in an idiom resembling the use of language by foreign workers. In his 'spoken opera' *Aus der Fremde* (*From Abroad*) all the characters speak exclusively in the subjunctive. 'Nonsense, as a conscious deviation from the logic of everyday language and purposeful thinking, represents a rejuvenating force that delays decay even if it doesn't prevent it' (*Anmerkungen zur Dichtkunst, Gesammelte Werke*, vol. iii, p. 620).

Daniil Kharms (Daniil Ivanovich Yuvatchev; 1905–1942), Russian writer of the absurd whose works, with the exception of his children's books, became known only posthumously. Since the 1960s, his 1939 collection *Cases* has appeared in many languages. In 1917, with Alexander Vvedensky and Nikolai Zabolotsky, he founded the Oberiu group, which was banned by the Soviet State in 1930. Kharms died in prison during the siege of Leningrad. It contributes to the absurdity of his texts that they are frequently pointless.

Velimir Khlebnikov (1885–1922), leading poet of the Russian avant-garde. With Vladimir Mayakovsky and Aleksei Kruchenykh he founded the Futurist group Gileas in 1912. Jointly with Kruchenykh he invented the artificial language Zaum. Khlebnikov was poor and had no fixed abode. His 'Poem of Laughter' emerged as an icon of modern poetry.

Christian Morgenstern (1871–1914), German poet, translator and editor. There are people who seem alive only when they smile or laugh. Morgenstern's serious, in part anthroposophic, poetry is forgotten while his *Galgenlieder* (1903) and the finest of his other grotesque poems have retained their freshness. To German literature, they added a missing dimension. An Esperanto version of *Palmström* was issued in 1983 in Paderborn. *Galgenlieder*, trans. Max Knight (University of California Press, 1964).

Illustrations

Man Ray, *Le Cadeau* (*The Gift*), *c.* 1958
Museum of Modern Art (MoMA), New York
Photo: Paige Knight/SCALA, Florence

Kurt Schwitters, *Konstruktion für edle Frauen* (*Construction for Noble Ladies*), 1919
Los Angeles County Museum of Art (LACMA)
Photo: © bpk / Los Angeles County Museum of Art (LACMA) / Art Resource, NY

Kurt Schwitters, *Mz 334 Verbürgt rein*, 1921
Marlborough Fine Art (London) Ltd
Catalogue: *Kurt Schwitters*, The Tate Gallery (London)/ Museum of Modern Art (New York), 1985

Dada Universal, graffiti, 2016
Landesmuseum Zürich
Photo: Maria Majno

Francis Picabia, *Edtaonisl* (*Ecclesiastic*), 1913
The Art Institute of Chicago
Foto bpk / The Art Institute of Chicago / Art Resource, NY.
Catalogue: *Our heads are round so our thoughts can change direction*

Francis Picabia, *Parade amoureuse*, 1917
Mr and Mrs Morton G. Neumann
Catalogue: *Francis Picabia*, Städtische Kunsthalle
Düsseldorf/ Kunsthaus Zürich

Hannah Höch, *Aus der Sammlung: Aus einem
ethnographischen Museum* (*From the Collection: From an
Ethnographic Museum*), 1929
Scottish National Gallery of Modern Art, Edinburgh
Photo: Antonia Reeve
Catalogue: *Hannah Höch*, Whitechapel Gallery, London/
Prestel Verlag, München, 2014

Franco Fedeli, *Lady from Arezzo*
Private collection
Photo: Maja Bodenstein

Acknowledgements

The essays 'Everything and Nothing: Dada 2016' and 'Schubert's *Winterreise*' first appeared in modified versions in the *New York Review of Books*. 'The Lady from Arezzo' was written for *Die Zeit*.

My warmest thanks go to Jill Burrows, Richard Stokes, Michael Morley, Misha Donat and Maja Bodenstein for their linguistic assistance, and Jeremy Adler for attempting the impossible in dealing with the translation of the untranslatable.

The translation of Velimir Khlebnikov's 'Incantation by Laughter' by Paul Schmidt is from Velimir Khlebnikov, *The King of Time*, trans. Paul Schmidt, ed. Charlotte Douglas (Harvard University Press, 1985), and of Christian Morgenstern's 'The Does' Prayer' by Max Knight is from Christian Morgenstern, *Galgenlieder*, trans. Max Knight (University of California Press, 1964).